WHY DON'T I HAVE ANYTHING TO WEAR?

WHY DON'T I HAVE ANYTHING TO WEAR?

Spend less. Shop smarter.
Revolutionise your wardrobe.

Andrea Cheong

Lagom

First published in the UK by Lagom
An imprint of Bonnier Books UK
4th Floor, Victoria House, Bloomsbury Square,
London, WC1B 4DA
Owned by Bonnier Books
Sveavägen 56, Stockholm, Sweden

Hardback – 978-1-788709-15-6
Ebook – 978-1-788709-16-3

A CIP catalogue of this book is available from the British Library.

Designed by Envy Design Ltd
Typeset design concept by Leigh John Maslij
Illustrations by Andrea Cheong
Printed and bound by Clays Ltd, Elcograf S.p.A

1 3 5 7 9 10 8 6 4 2

Lagom is an imprint of Bonnier Books UK
www.bonnierbooks.co.uk

You are worth it all

Contents

Introduction

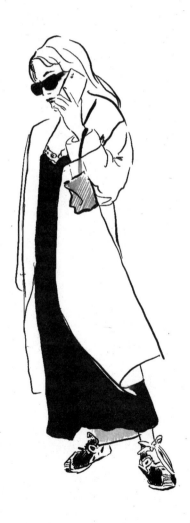

✦

Before reading this, you didn't know how to shop. It's OK – it's not your fault. I didn't used to know how to shop either.

For a minute, think back to every article you've ever read or video you've watched about how to do this. Reflect on every guide you've ever perused. The advice usually falls into the broad categories of styling, discovery or budgeting.

'Three Accessories to Go from Corporate to Date Night Attire'

'This Celebrity Favourite Vintage Boutique Just Opened'

'This Year's Top Black Friday Picks'

Almost every day of our lives we depend on monetary transactions – we can simply refer to it as 'shopping'. Open your online banking app and take a look at your statements; how many days in a row have you gone without any form of shopping whatsoever? Your groceries, your direct debits, taking the bus to work . . . You may not have considered something as mundane as an electricity bill as shopping but, at one point, you did compare deals and pick one. If you're spending money then you are shopping.

And yet shopping is often dismissed as a frivolous indulgence. It's also greatly gendered. We are quick to assume that it's a feminine pursuit. We think that women see it as a form of socialising, even a hobby, and that men aren't as susceptible to frittering money away. But studies show that men and women can and do shop as much as each other. It's just their approach and preference that differs. Research by Barclays Bank showed that British men spend more on clothes, shoes and grooming products each month compared to women and they would prefer to shop online rather than in store. Stephen J. Hoch, marketing professor at the University of Pennsylvania, noted that, 'Women think of shopping in an inter-personal, human fashion and men treat it as more instrumental. It's a job to get done.'[i]

So much research has been done on why we shop, how to get us to buy more and even what day of the week is most lucrative for retailers (Thursday, apparently). All of this and yet we have never *actually* learnt to shop. We learn every other basic life skill, like how to tie a shoelace or ride a bicycle (which I still can't do). It feels almost illegal that I stumbled across the realisation that we don't know how to shop for clothes. If we did, why do we always need to buy more?

For those that claim that they're not 'into fashion', shopping becomes intuitive and infrequent. These are small aspects of shopping more sustainably, some may argue. But it's not as simple as that. It's not just about spending money. Clothing is practical and not just in a protective way. It's a form of non-verbal communication. Those with strong styling skills or conversely, those who are the most prescriptive (for example, wear personal uniforms), are the most effective in conveying messages through their outfits. But we get so caught up in the struggle of learning how to do that that we lose sight of the foundation of shopping. And when we have no base knowledge or firm grounding, we are constantly lured into spending beyond our means or purchasing things that add no value to our lives.

'I'm an adult and I've gotten by just fine!' I hear you protest. I believe you. Some of us don't impulse buy. Some don't compulsively spend. Some don't have debt. Some don't experience guilt when they punch in their PIN numbers or sign a receipt. Some don't grip onto a scarcity mindset – a belief that there's not enough or an enhanced perception of what's missing in your life, which quickly becomes a focal point for anxiety. A major telltale sign that someone may suffer from this is when they are hyper fixated on absence, whether that's time, success or even a perceived lack of style.

I still think there's a lot for the financially confident among us to learn from this book. And that's because this isn't actually a book about money. This is a book about how to shop in the modern day. Climate change, socio-political turmoil, the reign of internet culture and a society where visuals dominate are all considered.

When we don't know how to do something, it leaves us at the mercy of those who would benefit from our ignorance. Don't know how to work out? The gym pockets your monthly membership and you still can't tell a dumbbell from a kettlebell. Don't know how to cook? You'll likely give yourself food poisoning and, before you know it, you're calling up delivery services more than you call your mum. In the case of shopping, it's the unscrupulous fashion brands who are the ones to gain. They will gladly take your money and, in return, give you a poorly made shirt derived from fossil fuels that's designed to fall apart. Best of all, they'll let you believe a healthy proportion of it is going to sweet old ladies in Asia.

An often-cited independent study claims that four out of five people favour brands with a positive approach to environmental sustainability,[ii] but the revealing figure is that nearly half of them don't understand what steps companies need to take to achieve this. This leads me onto the point that we have all tried, at least sub-consciously, to learn how to shop. As we've attempted to navigate being a 'conscious consumer', I bet you've heard the term 'buy less, buy better'. Frankly, I find that so annoying. My follow-up question is always, 'OK, but how?' If the person, brand or company who says this doesn't have an answer to that then it's just another marketing tool. A slogan to throw around. A hashtag that accompanies a branded post.

But I will tell you how. The premise is so incredibly simple that you may even laugh. If we knew how to shop, we would naturally be inclined to make better choices.

We would be more at peace with ourselves. In fact, if we knew how to shop, we wouldn't want to do it as much. And the best part is, this book is the last thing you'll need to buy to make that happen.

The Mindful Monday Method

If you've seen any of the Mindful Monday Method videos floating around on social media, you might think you know what it's all about. But there are several layers to it that are just not possible to get into in a short video format. Fashion may be the vehicle that I use, but the foundational lessons can be applied to any kind of consumerism. We're going to learn how to:

- ✦ Break unhealthy shopping habits learnt from childhood.
- ✦ Unlearn what pop culture (and the fashion industry) has taught us.
- ✦ Practise a new mode of shopping that benefits your wallet, mind and the planet.

Following these stages will help you unlearn the habits that fast fashion and social media have conditioned us to have for quick and dirty consumption. In relearning how to shop you'll realise that you're going to be incredibly discerning. Those who shop by my method say that because of it, there's a very small pool of what is available to buy. This is exactly the point I want to impress. I mean, it makes perfect sense that there's so little that's 'worth it' when so much fashion is unnecessarily produced!

Together, we are going to cut through that urge to impulse shop. We are going to take back control of how we spend and what we spend on. Retailers will tell you that shopping is empowering, but what is truly empowering is learning how to say 'no'. Put that papery polycotton shirt back on the rack and walk away. You deserve better.

How the Mindful Monday Method was created

If you met me in my twenties then I'm sorry, I was an asshole. For the majority of you who didn't have the displeasure, here's the context: I was what you'd call an 'influencer'. I've always cringed at that word. It fitted me like an underwired bra that was two sizes too small. The longer I wore it, the more uncomfortable it felt and the deeper a mark it left.

I constantly faced the conflict of needing to show newness and trends while being uneasy with the excess consumerism I was promoting. Then there was the other problem, one that is deeply entrenched in the fibres of the fashion and social media industry. I was fixated on building an 'image'. Of what exactly, I wasn't sure. I just crossed my fingers and hoped I'd figure it out along the way. After all, young people everywhere are seduced by the promises of the glamorous hustle culture, a twilight zone where name-dropping and spending beyond your means is just part of the job. Fake it until you make it, they say. Or until your last penny drops and not only do you have nothing to wear, but you also really hate yourself. Whoops, I overshared. But if I were you, I'd get used to it.

When I was cultivating the Mindful Monday Method, the 'mindful' part was always going to be integral. Mindfulness is about being self-aware and conscious, with a great leaning towards our wellbeing. The fact is, if we don't feel good about what we're choosing, buying and wearing as we 'do life', we're ignoring an enormous part of what helps us to function daily. Throughout this process of learning to shop, mindfulness is what we will always return to. And whatever the fashion dilemma, you'll learn to fall back on the knowledge I'll impart. As you practise it, you'll start to become attuned to that gut feeling that accompanies insight. But I can't go further without the aforementioned oversharing. I'm going to have to tell you a bit more about myself. It was the struggles I faced that led to the creation of this shopping method. After all, isn't there an old adage about solutions and problems? If you know the one I'm talking about, feel free to let me know.

So, before we get into how I became professionally equipped to create this method, let's get personal. I struggled with an eating disorder in my teens and anxiety and depression throughout my adult life. And then, at age 30, I discovered that I also have ADHD.

A few years ago, I had a severe mental health crisis. The kind that changes your life forever. The kind where you wish you weren't around anymore. It sparked this deep, burning desire to change. I went to therapy. I found my faith. I started volunteering – at first, when-ever I was free, now, every week if I can. I have come to see my experiences over the last couple of years like personality rehab. I can honestly say that I'm a very different person to the miserable cow you might've interacted with when I was in my twenties.

To start with, I discovered two things that sparked the beginning of the Mindful Monday Method – which is, to my knowledge, the only comprehensive guide teaching you how to shop in the digital age. First, I realised I couldn't be a 'fashion influencer' in the same way I had been. Not just in what I was sharing, but the mindset that accompanied it. Spending the equivalent of a month's rent on fulfilling a shoe addiction is, in fact, not a vibe. I'm looking at you, Carrie Bradshaw. Second, I also made a profound discovery that is also rather countercultural. It may even go under the heading 'Most Unpopular Opinions Ever'. My realisation was that I had to stop pursuing happiness. We can buy dopamine hits but we can't buy real happiness. Deep down we know this, yet we still like to think we can put a number on it – *if I make this much, I'll be so comfortable that I'll be happy.*

The secret was to change the goal from seeking happiness to seeking peace.

After this, everything started to fall together. Peace is

often pitched as the antidote to a life of fun. This is entirely untrue. When you have peace, the world opens with wonder. It's as if someone's turned up the brightness, sharpness and saturation. It's like washing away the gunk that's accumulated like a film of limescale over life. Tranquillity is a hard state to find, but I believe that's because of the culture that we live in, as opposed to it being unattainable.

Everything about our world is anti-peace. More likely than not, you'll consider 'peacefulness' to be boring. The problem lies in what we've been conditioned to prioritise over serenity. Drama and online gossip are seen as exciting, when really they're destructive and often too binary to produce any meaningful outcome. Reality TV encourages us to be far too emotionally invested and spikes our cortisol. You may feel you've forgotten your problems while rich housewives are slinging water across the table, but when the credits roll and the screen goes black, how do you feel?

There's also the belief that peace has a high barrier to entry. It could even be considered as a classist concept. It's also closely aligned with meditation, fasting and the realm of spirituality. Depending on what your preferences are, this can be off-putting. But it doesn't need to be elitist or otherworldly. Money can be exchanged for flights of happiness but it can never buy any amount of peace. Like death, peacefulness is one of the great equalisers of the world. Secondly, mindfulness doesn't need to involve any magic. It doesn't require rituals or accessories. I would even argue that the commodification of so many wellness products is counterproductive to the very concept of finding peace.

The Mindful Monday Method won't make you happy. To be honest, you'll probably be quite frustrated in the beginning. But it will be a tool in eventually finding peace through perfecting the art of (not) shopping.

How am I qualified?

One of the questions I receive the most is how do I have the experience and information that built the Mindful Monday Method? I can't claim to have had a particularly inspiring career before I found my purpose here. A few years ago, during the final stage of a job interview, a CEO of a fashion startup made me cry. She told me that I had no idea what I was doing with my life and that I should go back to being an influencer. No points for guessing that I didn't end up working there. However, the saying that everything happens for a reason has never rung truer.

You already know that I was a typical fashion influencer. Before that, I studied the history of art. It's one of those degrees people scoff at because they think I must either be a trust-fund baby who'd be funnelled into a Mayfair gallery upon graduation or an academic hipster. I am neither of those. I share that with you because what I did take away from my bachelor's degree was the ability to scrutinise objects and form an analysis. In this context, it is analysing clothes for how they are made, the quality and where this fits among the brand's competitors and eco claims. This became the rudimentary basis of the Mindful Monday Method.

I also worked in retail for a long time. This is where I learnt many of the tricks that retailers use to incite purchases. Everything from discount staggering, how products are displayed to hiring attractive sales assistants. I'm still susceptible to the fine inner workings of a beautiful store, but knowing the landscape has saved me from many unwanted visits to the cash register. This is what I'll share with you in the coming chapters.

One of the most interesting yet brief jobs I ever had was working at a trends agency. I soaked up all I could when it came to understanding consumer behaviour and what a 'trend' really is. It's a tool I used when creating the Mindful Monday Method because learning how to shop isn't an ideal to exist in a vacuum. It's a practical life skill that needs to address real problems.

Working for magazines taught me a lot about how commercially driven the mainstream media is. You probably suspected as much. I can literally feel you rolling your eyes at me right now. Still, unless you too are from this industry, you possibly don't understand just how much advertisers dictate the pages of a glossy or the homepage of a website. How symbiotic the relationship is between the publication and brands' publicists. Mainstream print media has played a ginormous role in how we obtained our shopping habits.

Despite trying my utmost to find a career path away from social media, the prodigal daughter returns. Let's be clear, I don't hate influencers. I've even made peace with the fact I'm still considered one. What I hate is the culture. What made it possible to slink back to the digital world was that I was greeted with open arms by a wonderful platform named TikTok. At the time, it was seen as a buzzy, mysterious app for teenagers to post dance videos. However, it became an invaluable platform for me to share educational fashion videos and less than a year into posting, I was able to focus on the Mindful Monday Method full-time.

I was able to do that because this method works.

These are just some of the comments and messages I've received from people telling me how this revolutionary way of shopping has changed their habits:

'Your method gives me extra filters to put my choices through which has already saved me so much money and time and guilt – so thank you.'

'I just wanted to say thank you, because I feel way more empowered to say no to items, and also more informed to know how to look for quality and environmental/ethical considerations thanks to your vids.'

*'So far this year you've saved me £494! Looking
for some work pieces, looking at labels is making
me much more discerning.'* (And I received this
at the end of January!)

*'You've changed my WHOLE approach
to shopping!'*

The journey of the Mindful Monday Method

This transformative way of shopping had humble beginnings. It began in 2019 as reviews of high street, cult designer and luxury collections. It happened every Monday on social media, where I would share my review of a selection from one or two brands. At first, I was motivated by a desire to understand why I was spending so much on clothes yet never had anything to wear. I would turn garments inside out, check the finishes on hems, scan sleeves for signs of damage and read care labels to decipher fibre compositions. All for the goal of understanding the price and quality axis.

I know that this is something you've thought about before. Every time you murmured, 'That was a rip-off' or 'That is way too expensive for what it is', but couldn't explain why, you were trying to evaluate quality. The thing is, you were never given the vocabulary or foundations to flesh out the inkling that something wasn't quite right. And when you've got a top in your cart for £19.99 that looks like something your favourite celebrity wore last week, it's easy to push the idea out of the way that this just isn't worth it.

A few months into the reviews, I began to realise it all went deeper than whether or not a jumper was fairly priced. As consumer consciousness around how fast the trend cycles are becoming and how much people were buying increased, the more companies took advantage. Brands saw sustainability as a trend to capitalise on. They sought out the quickest route to align themselves to the environmental cause. I was intrigued by the discrepancy between what was advertised and what was disclosed on the garment through its labels.

As those who are familiar with the method will have heard before, I always say 'the swing tags are the head-line, the story is in the care label'. You wouldn't claim to know a news piece if you only scanned the title. And once you got to read what those labels had to say, you wouldn't want to buy it anymore. It's no surprise that a 2021 report by the Changing Markets Foundation found that 60 per cent of claims of UK and EU fashion companies had no basis and were deceptive.[iii] The Mindful Monday Method took on a second purpose: to teach people to break their reliance on brands and be empowered to shop for themselves.

OK, we're on the same page. But how did we get here and how do we leave?

I have a feeling that our shopping habits are formed much earlier than we think. Like many tweens, I thought that having a floor-to-ceiling walk-in wardrobe meant I had made it. I'm thinking of that closet reveal moment in *The Princess Diaries* that really marks the beginning of Mia's transformation from an unpolished, outcast teenager into a princess. As an adult, I thought that I could buy myself a new life – even for just a day – with a new outfit. I could morph into a new person, perfectly accepted and perhaps even admired, with the help of my fairy godmother: a Visa card.

It's a fantasy I see perpetuated every time I open a social media app and see endless fashion hauls and try-ons geared to every occasion imaginable, including your neighbour's cat's funeral. We've observed shopping patterns that play on our insecurities in our personal experiences, advertising, pop culture, you name it. They're habits we've rehearsed from the moment we received our first payslip.

At time of writing (2023), it's been four years since the Mindful Monday Method was conceived. Along the way, I've learnt invaluable things about the fashion industry. The kind of things that they simply don't (and won't) teach you at school. Things that only insiders know from working in a very dirty industry. I've used all I've gleaned from brands, factory owners, designers, influencers, public relation contacts and magazine editors. The Mindful Monday Method is constantly evolving as new innovations, data and information emerge, but the core values that drive the five steps stay the same:

+ Knowledge is empowering; spending is not.
+ Mindfulness or peace cannot be bought.
+ Judging yourself and others prevents us from making progress.

Now that you know how it all started and what it's all about, we can't go much further without addressing the Covid-19 pandemic. At the time of writing, we are only just uncovering the true impact of one of the most historic events of my generation's lifetime. You only need to look at the rising cost of clothes impacted by shipping prices, soaring energy prices and workforce crises, for a glimpse of deeper issues.

The aftershock of lockdowns, restrictions and job insecurity has revealed the enormous shortcomings of the fashion industry. For many brands, old and new, supply chain issues were rife. Workers were laid off as retailers cancelled orders worth millions of dollars, some of which remain unpaid. Clean Clothes Campaign (CCC) is a non-profit that fights against the injustices suffered by workers within fashion's supply chain. It reports that wage theft by fast fashion brands equates to about 11.85 billion USD in unpaid income and severance from March 2020 to March 2021.[iv] Wage theft is a form of exploitation that refers to the practice of unfairly paying employees for their labour, whether that's through inadequate compensation or withholding financial remuneration. It's cheating and everyone knows, cheating isn't cute. Yet H&M group, one of the companies often cited by the CCC, reported an increase of 11 per cent in local currencies in the fourth quarter of 2021 alone.[v]

I believe that given the choice between kindness and apathy, most of us would choose the first. We don't make 'unethical' purchases because we're assholes. I mean, those people definitely exist, but I'm sure it's not you. We do it because we don't know how to shop. It's the divide between why we buy and who we want to be that this method aims to reconcile.

On the environmental side, who remembers those hopeful news stories of cleaner air? It was reported that during the first worldwide lockdown in 2020, China, Italy, France and Spain saw a 20–30 per cent reduction in nitrogen dioxide emissions, a noxious gas that is emitted primarily through fuel burning.[1] It took so much loss, devastation and a complete pause in our busy lives to realise that slowing down could be the simple solution to repairing environmental damage.

The global cost of living crisis that has soared in the aftermath of the pandemic has forced us to reconsider what is of value. We are now concerned not just with convenience and aesthetics, but what's good for the planet and good for our wallets. Underpinning all of that is reflecting on what's also good for our mental health.

Now you're clued up to the point where we can actually discuss the five steps of the method. The first thing people want to know is 'where can I shop?'. The long answer will be clear once you've finished the last page of this book. The short answer makes me rather unpopular in the sustainable fashion circles. It's that you can shop wherever you need to. 'Need' is the operative word. That's because no one else but you understands your geo-social, economic or emotional situation. Certainly not me. But first, I ask you to follow all five stages, covered in the following chapters, so you can make the most informed decisions.

The first step is a **wardrobe audit**, which will help you discern your personal style and separate need from want. And if you so desire, it'll also aid in carving out a real capsule wardrobe, without starting from scratch and without spending any money.

The second one is a **budget review,** which will ask you, 'are you comfortable with how much you spend on fashion per month?'. We'll go through some tips on how to shop less and make the most of what you have.

The third on the programme is to **outline your sustainability goal**. Daunting, but don't worry, I'll help you out with that.

Next, we will learn about **material composition**, its environmental impact and what to look for.

The fifth and final step is what I think is the most overlooked aspect of sustainable fashion: **quality**. It's about understanding that price doesn't mean better made and knowing what to accept and expect from retailers. For example, a cut corner to increase profit margins versus intentional design.

These five steps are the key to saving money and doing better for the planet. But here's your warning: once your eyes have been opened, you can't unsee.[vi]

This method is for everyone, no matter which 'conscious brands' you like, how much you care about the orangutans in Indonesia or if you even know what 'sustainable' means.

You're here because there's a part of you that wants to change how you shop. You're sick of having nothing to wear but always feeling stretched at the end of the month – even with a stuffed wardrobe and that one chair we all have in the corner of our room that's heaving with clothes. Some part of you knows that how we've been consuming fashion has significant power to harm us. Perhaps it already has.

Why do I never have anything to wear?

There is an indiscriminate issue that has plagued us since the beginning of time and we cannot stand for it any longer. No, it's not having to set an alarm for work. It's worse. It's feeling like we never have anything to wear. It's that frustrated desperation that ensues as we tip half the contents of our wardrobe onto the floor. The most harrowing part of this experience that unites us all is cleaning up. OK, but in all seriousness, it's realising that hundreds, if not thousands of pounds worth of textile, is lying at your feet.

My reason for not having anything to wear begins with my very complicated relationship with clothes. Growing up in an Asian household, my dress size was not my personal business. It was also my family's and their friends' remit. This only stoked the fire that was an eating disorder and body dysmorphia in my teenage years. No amount of living off chewing gum and cranberry juice for weeks at a time would hold off the comments about how chubby I was or how I thought I had a muffin top. I imagined myself as svelte and graceful, what I was told Chinese girls should be. But this never translated when I looked in the mirror. Getting dressed was torturous. It was a constant reminder of how far from acceptable I was. And I saw that echoed in the media, everywhere I looked.

My generation grew up with the trope of the 'out-of-place girl striving for a career at a publication but never fitting in'. Think of the hit US TV show *Ugly Betty* and the iconic romcom *13 Going on 30*. Oh, and the most legendary of them all, *The Devil Wears Prada*. Celebrities like Paris Hilton and the Olsen twins were not simply celebrated for their amazing sense of style, the media both criticised and glorified their low BMI. It was a bizarre and brutal time, and, as many millennials can attest, we are still healing from those toxic influences.

Fashion can be used as a tool for acceptance but it can also be a damaging experience, especially for women. Having walked both paths, the good and the bad, I have a personal and vested interest in helping you heal your relationship with yourself and shopping. Think of it as fashion therapy. The best way to get stuck into the enormous subject of why we have nothing to wear is to begin with a quiz. Because why not?

I encourage you to read the answers of the results that don't apply to you for a thorough understanding of how the fashion industry works.

What shape did you mark the most?

Find your shape below to help you understand the reason behind why you might have nothing to wear.

Recent weight fluctuation

Most of my clothes are uncomfortable

I'm unsure what my style is

I have too many clothes

My wardrobe is disorganised

I'm unsure what's age appropriate

I don't know where to shop

My clothes don't represent me

My clothes don't tend to last

Everything I have looks the same

Brands don't cater to my physical needs

The clothes I want are too expensive

I've moved country

I have trouble styling my clothes

I'm unsure what's appropriate for formal occasions

Not enough plus size options

Not enough tall/ petite options

I'm bored easily

My clothes make me feel self-conscious

I've just had a baby

My storage sucks, I can't see all my clothes

I'm not sure what's worth spending on

Change in lifestyle/job

I buy a lot of trends/different aesthetics

Most of my clothes are statement pieces

Triangles: Your physical needs aren't being met by mainstream brands

Before we begin, we need to understand the way that fashion production works. The first thing you need to know is that this is a 'them' problem, not a 'you' problem. Brands are not good at catering to bodies that don't align with industry average measurements. This is a systematic issue. A friend studying pattern making at university commented that they aren't educated on how to design for curvy bodies, which is the crucial starting point for making clothes. And as you can imagine, if mainstream fashion education doesn't even include the vast majority of society from the get-go, not only does not catering for larger sizes become entrenched as the norm but it's even harder to confront.

All garments start with a pattern (a sewing template if you will). This is a technical drawing that is sent to a factory. If the factory is Fully Factored (FF), also known as Full Package Production (FPP), this is a one-stop shop where they will source the fabric and create the garment for the client. If it's a Cut Make Trim (CMT), the operation is usually slightly smaller and focuses on creating the clothes. Designers will have to send fabrics and specifications for production. Next, the pattern is graded for various sizes, often starting from UK 6/US 0 up to UK 16/ US 14. The difference between them is about 5cm. The fabric is cut and sewn. Once the 'toile', or sample, is made up, it undergoes rounds of fittings and amendments.

Fast fashion brands intentionally miss the process of multiple fittings as they prioritise the lowest price point possible. And whatever takes more time costs more money. So when you come across styles like bodycon, oversized fits and, in some instances, even techniques like shirring, at first it seems like you're getting a 'good deal'. When fashion brands give us trending styles for lower prices, it's natural to think that it's value for money. And sometimes, when it's done well, it can be. But that's only discernible when you understand the commercial decisions behind each of the items on that rack. Then you might realise that it wasn't an innocent design choice or necessarily made to benefit us at all. For example, many bodycon styles rely on stretchy materials over complex patterns. Oversized outfits are marketed as 'relaxed', so customers are less likely to feel the need to return them as they're meant to look too big. And shirring (or known as 'smocking' in some regions. Although, in the UK, this refers to needlework that cannot currently be replicated by machine) – the use of elastic thread in several lines to create a scrunched pattern – can be an economical way to reduce fittings as it lends a great degree of stretch. This is not to say we should avoid any of the above examples, it's about buying style with substance through learning about how to shop for quality fashion.

Manufacturing for the average body also applies to height. Fit models are often five foot five and upwards for mass-market brands and about five foot seven for premium and luxury retailers. So those who consider themselves petite or tall will struggle with things like the length of sleeves, crotch length (which matters for both back and front measurements) and awkward hemlines.

I spoke to Abisola Omole, the CEO and creative director of Studio Arva and a social media content creator. She's known for speaking out against diversity and inclusivity issues in the British fashion industry in order to raise awareness and a lot of the time it's for the educational benefit of brands. 'The whole point of awareness is obviously for it to lead to change,' she says. The good news is that advancements have been made, Abi adds, 'it definitely has changed a lot [over the last few years]. But it's not where it needs to be. It needs to be at a place where it's just like, like for like, it's just normal', as opposed to plus sized bodies having a different experience when it comes to shopping. Other positive news is that brands are starting to address the other giant elephant in the room – planned obsolescence.

In-house repairs and alterations may soon become the norm in all major stores. It's brilliant in theory, as a band-aid to the high volume, low cost and cut corners approach that the vast number of mass market brands take. In reality, it should take place alongside a higher standard of garment production, particularly for brands that are direct to customer, as opposed to operating on a wholesale model, as they are more likely to have a larger profit margin. Although, some might tell me that this is idealistic. While it may seem like a completely new offering and quite a challenge, the infrastructure isn't alien. This has been far more common in premium menswear shops than women's. In fact, online startups like the UK-based Sojo have raised 2.4 million USD in seed funding.[vii] The aim is to work with retail giants to offer repairs en masse, so that the brands themselves are responsible for repairing and altering clothes. It's easier to make positive changes in the name of sustainable fashion faster when you're building this into a retailer's infrastructure. It's simpler for customers to deal directly with the store that they bought from and lends to making brands more responsible for the tons of clothes that they produce.

I'm a huge advocate for learning basic sewing skills. It's a cost-effective way to improve the wearability of our clothes. But for those who can't think of anything worse than threading a needle in their spare time, there are digitised repair services, like apps and websites that help to connect people with tailors in their area. It's worth noting that these are still challenging businesses for startup owners to navigate. The very nature of anything that goes against the current will undoubtedly face rockier seas. An example of this is The Restory, an industry darling and one of the true originals for luxury repairs. They had partnerships with the likes of luxury marketplace Farfetch and Harvey Nichols. In 2023, they went into administration. So while the volume of content around sustainability in the media and on social platforms may make it seem as if we're riding the peak of the zeitgeist, in reality we are just embarking on the journey. The growing interest in sustainability and what even qualifies as 'sustainable' is still in its infancy.

A major reason for returns is poor fit. ASOS is a company that suffers from high levels of return requests and in 2018, they launched the 'Fit Assistant' to suggest the best sizes for customers, based on what they already own. Unsure if you're a medium or large? Its recommendations are based on what others with similar body stats to you decided was best for them.

In the US, tech companies such as TrueFit are employed at places like PacSun, Lululemon and Madewell, who all share the same desire to instil customers with more confidence to check out. TrueFit is an artificial intelligence driven fit advisor that asks shoppers to identify a brand that they've worn before and feel confident that they have the correct size in. The technology looks at the various measurements and feedback on clothing and footwear across multiple brands to recommend the sizes for you, depending on the desired fit. Solutions like these help both the retailer and the customer.

I don't know about you but the thought of having to package a return, fill out a form and haul a bag to the nearest post office is a logistical headache. The amount of people I see with garment bags in the queue at a post office on a lunch break . . . But it's not just about being a chore. Returns also have a negative impact on the environment.

We're not just talking about packaging or the carbon

emissions from the transport. What's arguably more pressing is how brands save time (and therefore money) by discarding returns instead of sorting through them. This is a manual job that requires meticulous attention to spot any soiling, faulty hardware or damages.

Since 2022, fashion retailers have begun to reject the status quo of providing free returns. The benefit of stopping free returns in the name of sustainability is shaky and it's generally acknowledged to be a cost-saving tactic. But while I'm firmly in the camp that manufacturing and delivering clothes of an acceptable standard is the responsibility of companies and the government, that doesn't mean that conscious shoppers are completely helpless. It's possible to reduce the number of trips you have to take into stores with a crumpled receipt in hand.

Here are my suggestions for a toolkit to make shopping a little less overwhelming:

Invest in measuring tape so you can take note of your size and compare it against the measurements on the websites. I've only ever come across a handful of brands that have neglected to include this detail on their e-commerce, so this should be widely accessible. If not, a simple email to customer service will usually sort you out.

Understanding your 'image identity'. At the risk of verging on personal style advice (which the Mindful Monday Method doesn't focus on), familiarising yourself with your proportions can really help with keeping your clothes for longer and shopping with confidence.

Introduction

New York stylist David Kibbe invented the idea of 13 body types, back in the eighties. If you haven't heard of it already, it's all about dressing in harmony with your body. What I appreciate is that this approach focuses on your 'essence', facial features and the lines of your physique. In theory, bodies of every shape and size could gain from a template of how to dress in a conventionally 'flattering' way, if they so wished.

The book, *David Kibbe's Metamorphosis: Discover Your Image Identity and Dazzle as Only You Can*, has been out of print for a few years, but thanks to viral videos on social media where commentators use it to type celebrity style, Kibbe has experienced a huge resurgence in interest. While it has faced criticism for not being inclusive enough with its examples, I see it as more the fault of the times rather than a flaw in the system itself. Fortunately, fans today are giving it a much-needed update, showing how it can apply to a far wider size and shape range.

There are plenty of free resources online, such as YouTube videos, digestible examples on TikTok, forums and blog posts about discovering where you fit in. Even if you decide not to get formally assessed through hiring an image consultant, reading about how different silhouettes and styles work can really curb impulse buying or FOMO over microtrends that we really don't need to buy into!

Understanding your colour palette has been the best piece of style advice that's helped me dress myself better. This has also seen a boom in popularity thanks to social media. If you haven't heard of it before, it's based on colour theory and has its roots in art. First, Bauhaus artist Johannes Itten created the concept of four colour palettes to complement the complexions of subjects in portraits. Second, Suzanne Caygill formalised the notion that there's a link between personality and a person's colours/tones. Then, in the 1980s, Carole Jackson's bestselling book, *Colour Me Beautiful*, popularised seeing the four main colour palette as the seasons – you could be a spring, summer, autumn or winter. What started as a book has now grown into a huge network of trained specialists and image consultants that can analyse your season for you.

Again, it's fine if you don't feel this is something you need to do formally or even live by, but simply acknowledging the way colours can enhance or subdue physical characteristics is a basic aspect of personal styling. Being able to gauge what hues best suit you is so beneficial to those of us who are trying to shop less. It can increase your discernment as you shop, so for example, if a particular shade of blue starts to pop up everywhere and you're on the fence about it, knowing that it's far from flattering your tone makes it easier to resist temptation. Plus, it can also lead to holding onto a garment for longer simply because you know you look good in it, regardless of trends.

The ultimate rebellion against fast fashion is to not invest in clothes but ourselves. Another option is to go for brands that offer totally bespoke sizing and measurements. I spoke to Patricia Luiza Blaj, the founder behind the slow fashion brand Loud Bodies. Her career didn't start with fashion design school or pattern cutting – she wanted to be a fashion writer but ended up blogging instead. Facing prejudice in the industry, she was often paid much less than her peers and felt like a token for diversity when it came to advertising campaigns. In 2018, she launched her brand with just a seamstress. It didn't begin with the goal of being sustainable.

If you really think about it, an ethical business is the strongest foundation for creating a sustainable brand. Blaj tells me succinctly, 'Sustainable fashion starts with the people – both those buying the clothes and those making clothes. People always say, "Oh, sustainability is so complicated, there are so many certifications, there are so many shades of grey." You can start with the people. There are no shades of grey there: you either pay a living wage or you don't. That's literally where everybody should start. If you cannot pay those who make your clothes a living wage you shouldn't have a business.' It's a statement that is so simple you can't help but be surprised by its truth.

Loud Bodies caters to those who are often under-served by mainstream fashion. The made-to-order brand is based in Romania and offers customisation of hemlines, pockets (or no pockets), ranging from size XXS to 10XL in a variety of materials, many of which are lower impact and not your typical stretch fabrics that fast fashion companies have convinced us are needed for larger bodies. 'It's about caring about fat bodies enough to make clothes for them. I do not think it's limiting in any way or that the fabrics are a challenge. I think it's biases that are limiting,' Blaj explains.

It's brands like these that are spotlighting the inadequacies of mainstream offerings. It is not financially viable for most of us to choose a bespoke piece every single time we need a new article of clothing. But Blaj's clothes aren't based on everyday pieces. So for those times when we know we'll part with a significant sum, that seems like the perfect time to vote with our wallets and choose an independent, slow fashion business instead of a faceless label.

Squares: You're undergoing a lifestyle change

When we undergo a lifestyle change and don't have the wardrobe to match, it feels like we're starting from scratch. This may seem like a fun problem to have but the financial cost can be overwhelming, not to mention it's even harder when we're trying to be more sustainable with our consumption.

In my early twenties, I moved from a three-year stint

in Singapore, where it was summer clothes all year round, to the UK and its very temperamental seasons. At the time, I was living off savings and working part-time while trying to find a fashion internship. I didn't have the funds to expand my wardrobe for single-digit winters, especially with how costly knitwear and outerwear can be. It constantly felt like I was throwing money down a hole, purchasing things that weren't ideal but 'good enough'.

I was always dissatisfied with my purchases. I'd carry them home in branded paper bags with a sense of guilt, like I was concealing polyester fugitives. As soon as the blouses and dresses found their way into my wardrobe, they'd stay locked up with limited visitation rights to the outside world. The worst part is I was barely fulfilling my needs because I didn't know how to shop. I thought I'd be able to shop better if I was rich. Now I know this wasn't the problem.

Then there's the challenge of body changes. A common question I get asked around this is, 'Should I wait until I lose weight to invest in better clothes?' My answer is always no. No matter what size you are, you're the same person. You deserve to be comfortable and feel confident in your clothing. We don't have to go out and buy an entire new wardrobe but we can definitely pick out core pieces for whatever season we're in.

As for those who have just become mothers, congratulations! Buying new clothes is probably the least pressing thing on your to-do list. But it's still important, so let's keep it simple. You may find that once you've given birth, your maternity clothes aren't suitable and your pre-mum wardrobe may not fit or be practical for things like baby vomit and feeding times. Yum. Another point of frustration is learning to dress your new body shape. It doesn't always have to do with 'gaining weight' but ribcages, hips and busts expanding for good. It can be emotionally taxing to accept this and also to feel like you've got to watch your favourite clothes gather dust.

It's most essential for you to spend time in the **wardrobe audit**, coming up in the next chapter. As you'll soon discover, this isn't about personal style but putting your lifestyle needs first. Fashion shouldn't get in the way of how you want to live your life – it's there to serve you. A query mothers have when it comes to the audit is whether they need to say goodbye to every single party dress that they owned pre-natal. The audit makes room for those old lovers that you might like to say hi to every now and then. What's critical is separating these from clothes that you wear daily and keeping them in storage. What you need should stay in prime sight because for now, the focus is a high-functioning wardrobe. In fact, this is also the beginnings of a very sustainable approach to dressing. Clothes are made to be worn and should serve you, not be admired inside the dark altar of your closet.

Circles: We need to practise mindful consumption

When we feel frustrated, bored or even resentful of our wardrobes – the very thing that is supposed to express who we are – we turn to retail therapy as real therapy. Trust me, it's not cheaper. I've tried both.

Another term for retail therapy could be 'impulse shopping'. Often, when we shop as a form of self-soothing, we don't really think about what we're about to purchase. Aside from feeling stretched thin each month, it also leads to other issues like not knowing how to style the mismatched items that you've found yourself saddled with. Thrill-seeking shopping brings a hit that's fleeting and has nothing to do with how good you feel about yourself afterwards. (In fact, it's often a negative reaction.) However, brands want to incite this emotion because before you know it, you'll need another hit.

When so much doesn't need to be made, there is so much we don't need to buy. This creates a very practical barrier that can really help to override those urges. But it can also give you the time and space to consider whether or not you really want to shop at all. Maybe, you're using it as a distraction from something else. I mean, we've all been there. I recommend spending most of your time in the journalling exercises in Chapter Two, which explores your relationship with spending.

Stars: Let's get you trained up to spot a quality piece

Planned obsolescence is the practice of designing a product that has a short lifespan with the aim of selling more to replace it. Combined with impulse shopping, this can really wreak havoc on our bank accounts. It's highly likely every single one of us can think of a time when something didn't live up to expectations because it fell apart after washing or was uncomfortable to wear. Learning how to spot quality pieces is this method's most pertinent takeaway for you.

Quality is also often associated with an item being expensive. This doesn't always have to be the case. The Mindful Monday Method reduces the risk of buying a pair of trousers with buttons that fall off after the first wear, no matter where you choose to shop. We just need to watch out for the telltale signs.

Refer to the guide to common red flags on the next two pages. These are collected since 2019, although I've tried to include the most recent examples from a sample of brands across all price points. It goes to show that price certainly doesn't guarantee that something is well made. It's worth remembering that a single one of these issues may not be a huge deal. We are not shopping for perfection. However, we know that it's a severe quality control concern if it's an issue that's almost impossible to fix. And we know it's something that we really don't need to waste our money on when the price vastly outweighs the this. Also, a combination of these red flags indicate

Examples of common issues

1 Sheerness can indicate cheaper or poorer quality fabric. It also limits versatility for the wearer.

2 Pilling on new items may suggest short and loose fibres, a lower-quality yarn or a delicate material that's high maintenance and unfit for mass production.

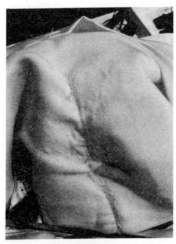

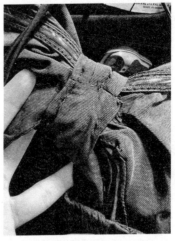

3 Bubbling between fabric and lining. Sometimes a sign of rushed production, where the fabric wasn't adequately prepped.

4 Uneven cutting of the fabric and messy stitches. The item may not last long if care is not taken during construction.

Examples of common issues

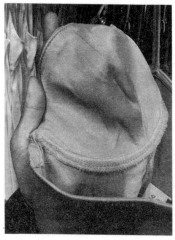

1 Wonky stitching along the underwire. The overall finishing with the exposed overlock is a sign speed is prioritised over quality production.

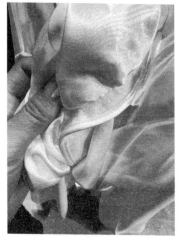

2 The ribbon (bias binding) isn't cut properly. The felt base that it covers is so large that it is easily exposed. Again, not sized correctly.

3 On the right of the panel, interfacing for the button area is visible. It should be concealed. This garment is by a luxury brand.

4 A buttonhole is coated in a plastic, perhaps for reinforcing the area. This should have been removed. This item's RRP is approx. £1,000.

that the garment may not last long. As we delve into understanding this, you'll be able to practice buying less but better with confidence.

Arches: Organisational issues

The **wardrobe audit** in the subsequent chapter is going to be your greatest help. Before I did mine, my sartorial real estate was always taken up by winter attire. Summer clothes tend to have less bulk and therefore they are stored folded up. Even on a hanger, they disappear when mixed in with knitwear, jackets and wool trousers. When you don't see what you have, it's hard to remember that it's there.

Have you ever noticed that when you're on holiday, it's much easier to get dressed? This is because you can see everything and it's completely relevant to where you are and what you'll be doing. I don't know anyone who would bring a down jacket to a tropical beach. So we should begin with curating what you have. We do this by separating your clothes by season, which immediately reduces how much is available to reach for. This also alleviates decision fatigue, which happens when you see too much you simply don't need.

When it comes to storage, always keep out-of-season items or miscellaneous things like ski clothes out of sight. These are occasional items that will naturally come to mind as and when you need them. I mean, who can forget that they own a wetsuit?

If possible, try not to keep your clothes in different

places for a long period of time. For example, at your parents' home, in a storage unit or in your sibling's attic. This should only be a stop gap; for example, if you're travelling the world for a few months or in between homes. Having your clothes completely out of sight and reach also means they're out of mind. This doesn't address the organisational issue that is a key part of why you feel you have nothing to wear. It may help you get dressed quicker in the mornings temporarily, but it's a band-aid. When you feel like shopping again, that space will fill up quickly and become cluttered. Then you're back to square one and running out of addresses that will house your clothing addiction. Take a look at Chapter Two, Money and Mental Health, for assistance.

Summary

✦ The fashion industry is not built on empowerment but learning to shop will correct that for you.

✦ There are five main reasons why we feel anxiety around shopping:

1. Your physical needs aren't met by mainstream brands – this is not a You problem.
2. You're undergoing a lifestyle change and unsure how to dress for it.
3. Impulse buying may be a problem; you tend to shop out of boredom or to fulfil another need.
4. You need to learn how to spot quality in clothing.
5. Organisational issues.

✦ You may have multiple reasons and these will change over time. Use the quiz whenever you feel the need to reassess your shopping habits.

✦ It is entirely possible to heal your relationship with spending and be confident in how you present yourself.

Chapter 1

T he first step in looking your best, feeling better and spending less is the wardrobe audit. I'll admit, to some it sounds as sexy as unpacking a suitcase. But it's integral in combatting that prickling sensation followed by a wave of nausea. I'm referring to spending guilt. Have you ever shopped when you're bored or stressed, or spent a little above your means? When we turn to retail therapy while we're feeling low, it's likely that after that little hit of dopamine subsides, we feel sick about our purchases, which leads to a vicious cycle of dissatisfied purchases.

When I asked my audience online if they ever feel like they have nothing to wear, they unanimously answered yes. So if you thought 'Fashion People' are immune to this affliction, you've been misled. Remembering that even the individuals that are viewed as tastemakers and experts feel this way may also be a helpful point whenever you feel self-conscious about your outfit – the truth is that everyone else is too busy worrying about theirs.

The second reason an audit is so important is that it allows you to see what you need to replace – not supplement – so that you are clear on what is a need versus a want. That's not to say that you have to deny yourself every cocktail dress that you chance upon; rather, it's about deciphering what the priority is when it comes to your shopping list. This will seriously help with budgeting, which comes up in our next chapter.

Now, I know not everyone is as obsessed as I am with videos of pantries being restocked (so satisfying) or gets delicious tingles from watching Marie Kondo say, 'thank you, next'. So I've made organisation and sorting through your clothes as pain-free for you as I can.

Task one: Create four piles

The wardrobe audit requires working within seasons, so think winter, autumn, spring and summer. It'll be a quicker job for those who live in countries with just one or two seasons. Lucky you. My preferred method of storage is vacuum pack bags if you're a little stretched for space. They reduce right down and are transparent, so it's easier to quickly identify what's in them.

First, we are going to create four piles. The first one is for the clothes that you still want but aren't in season. This is so whatever is visible in your wardrobe is relevant for the next few months. If you still find yourself reaching for a jumper in the summer, opt for a cotton knit. Pack away the thicker knitwear; save them for when the cold comes around again. At this point, be conscious of what marketing tells you is appropriate versus what you can actually wear. For example, linen is mostly sold in the summer but it's as versatile, breathable and chic as a classic cotton shirt. There's no reason not to wear that fabric all year round.

The second pile is for pieces that you can donate, gift to friends or sell. When it comes to donations, charity shops can receive thousands of items a week, many of which are in a poor state and cannot be sold. It's estimated that only 30 per cent of donations are actually sold in the UK.[viii] The majority is sent abroad to be another country's environmental disaster. We've all seen the ghastly images of the Atacama Desert in Chile and Kantamanto Market in Accra, Ghana. To mitigate this, use this tip: if you wouldn't feel comfortable giving it to a friend, it's not fit for resale. Instead, you may have to consider its potential for recycling. Pop it in the fourth pile.

It's also worth investigating what wouldn't be accepted by a charity shop in your country. Some common unwanted items may include:

+ Identifiable school and work uniform
+ Fur items
+ Body piercings
+ Underwear
+ Socks
+ Swimwear
+ Any blemished clothing, including light stains or small tears.

The third pile is for clothes that need to be repaired or altered. Home sewing is more than possible for many mishaps: putting buttons back on and adding a few 'security stitches' to plunging necklines are the simplest. Even jobs that look like they require a surgeon's touch – like tears in delicate fabric, particularly by the seams – are easily covered with a strip of lace or ribbon. Shortening cuffs and hemlines is relatively simple, provided there are no embellishments there.

However, if you're time-poor or the thought of a needle and thread is starting to stress you out, there are always tailors. Most local dry cleaning businesses in the UK will also offer basic tailoring services. Pricing will depend on where you live, how specialised the service is (many designer clothing fixes may end up costing a premium) and, of course, how complex the demand. It's worth factoring that maintenance into your shopping budget. So never consider the RRP as the final price. Think of each garment you buy as a responsibility. If you don't want the obligation, it's best not to shop it at all.

Being accountable for the items we already own will also help us be stringent when it comes to future purchases. For example, things like zips are more expensive to replace and I know it's so fiddly to do well on my own. Now that I'm aware of this, I pay particular attention to the quality of closures when shopping.

The fourth pile is for upcycling or, if that's not possible, recycling. Deciphering which items can be recycled can be slightly confusing but as a rule of thumb, synthetic blends are highly unlikely to be processed by mainstream facilities. Pieces that can be taken apart for new items need to be mono-fibre, for example, 100 per cent cotton or polyester (that being said, very few recycled polyester garments are currently made of other clothes and instead use plastic bottles).

Sorting clothes at recycling plants always begins with manual labour. The majority of recycling stations are currently lacking technology that can separate natural fibres that have been blended with synthetic ones. However, the good news is that since 2022, interesting innovations such as Valvan's Fibersort have been adopted by the Salvation Army Trading Company (SATCoL). The machine can tell the difference between different fabrics, even able to separate blends such as polycotton. For this it uses near-infrared spectroscopy cameras and for colour, RGB. Although humans are needed to discern whether donated clothing can be salvaged or is destined for recycling, the Valvan technology claims to be highly accurate, even able to break down percentages of fibres in a textile. At its early stages, it's currently processing 500 tonnes of textiles a year for the charity.

However, SATCoL reportedly receives around 50,000 tonnes of textiles annually and has 8,000 clothing collection banks located across the UK, holding up to 240kg of textiles.[ix] While it's commendable that we're able to treat 'waste' as the respectable resource it can be, this isn't a solution in and of itself. We'll discuss this a little more in Chapter Three, but for now, can we agree that the less we send to our recycling piles in subsequent wardrobe audits, the better?

Task two: Analyse what you no longer want

You've likely attempted to clear out your wardrobe more than once in your life and each time you seem to have had the same amount to toss out. This time it's going to be different because the focus is not on style and what you want to keep. Instead, we will be mainly focusing on what you don't want. This is a critical step in learning how to shop smart going forward.

Let's tackle pile number two first: donate and gift. I am hoping that you've followed my advice and not attempted to pass on the responsibility of a bobbling acrylic knit to your sister (yes, I see you). These should be clothes in good condition that you wouldn't be embarrassed to wear yourself. Most likely, they've made it into this pile because they don't fit you or reflect your tastes anymore. The analysis is the part that's really going to make the difference as it'll help you to understand your motivation for shopping. Tally up the pieces that correspond with the reasons below. Take a look at my example on the next page for guidance before you fill out your own audit. There are more suggestions for possible reasons on the next page to inspire your own conclusions.

For the items that need to be repaired or altered, we already have a solution: you're going to keep them and have them fixed. Let's get them back in your weekly circulation again!

Moving onto the fourth pile, we're going to uncover a lot more information. This is all about the clothes that you're ready to say goodbye to. Here, you'll want to see if any commonalities occur.

Suggestions for the 'Reasons' column of the audit:

1. Look at the labels. Do you find a particular material pops up again and again?

For example, when I did my first wardrobe audit, I realised I was purging a lot of polyester items because they made me feel sweaty and uncomfortable.

2. Are there any brands that appear numerous times? How many items from these brands are you letting go of?

If so, you now have proof that it doesn't serve you at all. Time to unsubscribe from those newsletters and sale alerts!

3. Is anything unsuitable for your lifestyle?

For example, delicate embroidery, silks, fine knits, etc.

4. Are you seeing a mishmash of aesthetics that aren't your style?

This could be a sign you need to focus less on dopamine-incentivised shopping that results in buying microtrends or perhaps you need more 'wardrobe staples'.

I've moseyed my way into many a wardrobe and the results are always interesting. Take the wardrobe audit I conducted with my friend Eva. She works in PR but is also an influencer. As you may have guessed, she owns a lot of clothes, many from brands that want to be featured on her social media platforms. Eva and I delved into the pieces she segregated for recycling and donation. The ones she didn't want anymore. At first, I was surprised. Her piles had a lot of cotton – even organic and recycled. As I inspected it, I quickly discovered that the issue was the quality of it.

Cotton is one of the most prevalent fibres used in fashion today. According to Cotton Inc, a non-profit that sits under the United States Department of Agriculture, 60 per cent of women's clothing items contain cotton fibres. From that small majority 40 per cent is entirely cotton. And even if it's natural or grown organically, there's a whole spectrum when it comes to quality.

The items that Eva wanted to be rid of were prone to colour transfer and sheer. She hated how they looked after one wash. Both of these issues indicate a quality problem, as opposed to something that's fibre specific. Dyes that aren't steadfast will fade quickly and fabrics that are see-through without a nice handfeel may have a low thread count and use shorter and fewer fibres. This is why they look translucent and feel rough. The sort-of-good news is that the items she no longer wanted were in the very least biodegradable. It's not ideal but should they ever end up in the landfill, they would have less of an impact on the environment than a fossil-fuel based fabric, which could take up to 200 years to degrade.

After the audit, Eva concluded that she no longer wanted to accept gifting based on aesthetics or how cool a brand is. It wasn't worth the responsibility of caring for so many items that weren't made to last. Nor did she want to add more of the same to her wardrobe. Five slip dresses are more than enough. And I think that realisation is worth a little applause!

The capsule wardrobe myth

You don't need to build a capsule wardrobe. There, I said it. This is because most likely, you already have one. It exists within what you already own.

A capsule wardrobe is a small collection of clothes that can be paired multiple ways with each other, including being dressed up or down. It's most commonly associated with a neutral colour scheme and a typically 'classic' style. The reality is that your true style is buried within sheaves of nondescript garments that you were cajoled into purchasing. All thanks to that clickbait article on the '5 Expensive-Looking Jumpsuits to Buy Now'. Understanding your most authentic personal taste outside of the influence of . . . well, influencers, is critical to shopping better and more sustainably. Let's unpick some common myths around the coveted 'capsule wardrobe'.

We need to address the idea that you have to start with a clean slate. A lot of this has to do with the media's perpetual messaging about building a timeless 'forever' collection. Often it's used as a marketing ploy to get you to buy more of the same. After all, there are only so many ways to sell the same camel overcoat every winter. Wanting an easy go-to selection of clothes that lasts for years to come is a brilliant idea, but not if it encourages you to question what's been working for you and throw everything out, only to copy the taste of a faceless editor. Or worse, a celebrity whose style you mostly see on the red carpet. Your wardrobe audit and the capsule wardrobe analysis below are going to help you uncover the essentials without spending any money.

The second myth is that a strong sense of style is based on repetition. When we look at examples like Karl Lagerfeld, whose glamorous monotone looks earned him an entire Met Gala theme, remember that these are public figures. Their outfits are an integral part of building a persona. While we can certainly borrow styling tips, the notion that we should emulate this isn't practical. If we are being realistic, how many of us need to be identifiable via the glimpse of fingerless gloves? If a uniform-like approach to dress gives you comfort, then that's great. It definitely makes getting dressed quicker in the mornings! But if you like the idea of it and have struggled to stay consistent, it may bring you relief to know that it's entirely unnecessary.

Another myth is that we all need the same base of clothes to work from. If fashion is truly about self-expression, why should we subscribe to this? Even on a practical level, this doesn't make sense. Take a smart suit, for example. If you're a music producer, your need for this is minimal, so investing in just one may suffice. But if you're a consultant working in the city, you may need multiple tailored sets. Everyone needs clean underwear and good shoes. Not everyone needs a pink mini dress for date night.

This next myth has a little more to do with looking put together. You may have heard the advice that when in doubt, go for black. Generally, I'd agree with this cheat code. However, the result is similar to my point that a restrictive wardrobe leaves us dissatisfied and possibly bored. If neutrals and dark colours aren't your thing, don't force it. In fact, University College London anthropologist Daniel Miller noted that 'wearers [of black] are often both more secure in their sense of the approval of others, but disappointed by their failure to attempt a more ambitious projection in the world'.[x]

Miller concludes that opting for black clothing is rooted in a desire for acceptance but represents a lack of individuality. It makes sense why it's so often the required dress code for roadies, hospitality workers and luxury sales assistants. These are situations in which staff aren't encouraged to draw attention to

themselves. Of course, this doesn't factor in subcultures and their love for black, such as goth and punk. But you probably realised that.

As much as I love an all-black outfit and sport plenty of them, I wanted to create a shopping method that would help the most timid of us to boldly explore other choices. With that, let's move on to how to shop from your own wardrobe, shall we?

How to find your capsule wardrobe

By now, you have made your four piles and analysed the clothes you no longer want. The majority of our wardrobe should be able to be used across all seasons. Let's aim for 70 per cent. These are wardrobe staples – the shapes, colours and styles that are a recurring go-to because they work for your lifestyle, needs and aesthetic. They vary with individuals, so don't fall into the trap of comparing yours to friends or family. The majority of people may feel that t-shirts, jeans and knitwear are their wardrobe staples, but if that's not you, that's not a problem. It's about how much you enjoy and how frequently you reach for those pieces.

Task one: A visual diary
Here's what you're going to do: for a week, every time you leave the house, take a mirror selfie of your outfit. If you're a homebody, you may need to stretch this to two weeks. You can add these photos to a new album on your

phone or 'favourite' the pictures, so you have something to easily refer to. The idea is to build a visual diary of approximately seven stellar outfits – a clear and concise visual of the clothes you feel comfortable wearing. If you know what works for you on a day-to-day basis, it can help fight the temptation to buy something you really won't wear much, that isn't 'you', especially if you find yourself browsing online 'just to see'.

If having a collection of these pictures is enough for you to feel confident with your collection, you've already done a great deal of work and can stop there.

Task two: Analysis

Stylists and fashion lovers argue over how many pieces should be in a 'true capsule wardrobe'. The consensus is around 25 but no more than 50 at a push. However, this is a detail that we don't need to obsess over but interesting to note when you do the task below and count how many items you actually wear over the course of a week.

The first part of the task provided a visual diary of outfits which makes it easier to get dressed and assures you that you actually do have a personal style! This next step is the analysis which will enable you to tailor the Mindful Monday Method to your lifestyle.

To help you do this, refer to the illustration of my seven outfits. The photos were taken during the spring months, so you'll see a bit of a mishmash of cool and warm weather outfits. Where I live, the weather can go from chilly and needing a light jacket to a heatwave in

24 hours. I favour high-waisted, wide-leg trousers and shorter hemlines. I'm petite, so these styles lengthen my legs and are more flattering on me than cropped hems or midi skirts. No matter what the ever-changing microtrends are, I will gravitate towards these proportions. I don't believe that every outfit needs to be

'flattering' as the main objective, but I do believe that once we learn the rules, we can break them and the coolest individual style comes from that kind of play.

Another point is focusing on the material composition of your ensembles. It's likely that you'll be working with a mix of fast fashion, vintage and even premium labels. If you find that you're pleased with the look of your seasonal capsule but you don't feel great in some of the items, use the same process in the wardrobe audit. Ask yourself:

✦ Is there a common retailer that pops up where I like the style but the fit and fabric causes discomfort?

✦ I like this item enough to hold onto it but it doesn't feel great. What is it made of?

If the need to replace a particular garment arises, it will be a planned purchase and so hopefully with much less spending guilt attached. This is because you already know it works with your wardrobe, you're conscious of what brand you're buying from and that the fabric is suitable for your lifestyle and sustainability goals. You can use the notes section of the template to record any thoughts such as these. Head to page 117 for the quiz on finding your sustainability goals.

This is how to find your capsule wardrobe and it didn't cost you a thing. You can use this every season or even when you sense your closet becoming cluttered and you need a reset. If you only get this far in learning

Why Don't I Have Anything to Wear?

My Capsule Wardrobe

Season: SPRING   SUMMER   AUTUMN   WINTER

No. of outfits:

No. of
different items:

Tops I've worn
the most:

WHAT I LIKE ABOUT IT	WHAT IT'S MADE OF

Bottoms I've
worn the most:

WHAT I LIKE ABOUT IT	WHAT IT'S MADE OF

Wardrobe Audit

One-pieces I've
worn the most,
e.g. dresses,
jumpsuits:

WHAT I LIKE ABOUT IT	WHAT IT'S MADE OF

Outerwear I've
worn the most:

WHAT I LIKE ABOUT IT	WHAT IT'S MADE OF

Notes:

how to shop, you already know a great deal more than you did yesterday.

Overleaf, I've also included a simplified decision tree for shopping for everyday clothes and another decision tree for occasionwear. This is meant as a guide with intentionally open-ended conclusions for some items. As we all know, there is no such thing as one-size-fits-all. The same goes for this. My hope is that you'll use it to carve out your own shopping standards based on your lifestyle, budget and sustainability goal. Try it next time you go shopping in real life and see what passes!

Shopping for everyday

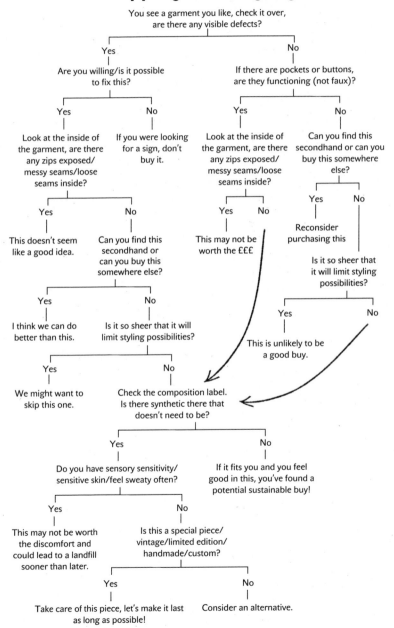

You see a garment you like, check it over, are there any visible defects?

Yes

Are you willing/is it possible to fix this?

Yes — Look at the inside of the garment, are there any zips exposed/messy seams/loose seams inside?

No — If you were looking for a sign, don't buy it.

Yes — This doesn't seem like a good idea.

No — Can you find this secondhand or can you buy this somewhere else?

Yes — I think we can do better than this.

No — Is it so sheer that it will limit styling possibilities?

Yes — We might want to skip this one.

No → Check the composition label.

No

If there are pockets or buttons, are they functioning (not faux)?

Yes — Look at the inside of the garment, are there any zips exposed/messy seams/loose seams inside?

Yes — This may not be worth the £££

No → Check the composition label.

No — Can you find this secondhand or can you buy this somewhere else?

Yes — Reconsider purchasing this

No — Is it so sheer that it will limit styling possibilities?

Yes — This is unlikely to be a good buy.

No → Check the composition label.

Check the composition label. Is there synthetic there that doesn't need to be?

Yes

Do you have sensory sensitivity/sensitive skin/feel sweaty often?

Yes — This may not be worth the discomfort and could lead to a landfill sooner than later.

No — Is this a special piece/vintage/limited edition/handmade/custom?

Yes — Take care of this piece, let's make it last as long as possible!

No — Consider an alternative.

No

If it fits you and you feel good in this, you've found a potential sustainable buy!

Shopping for occasionwear

An example of how to use the method

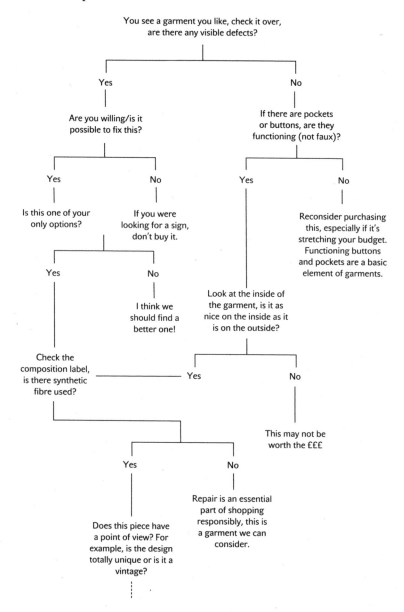

You see a garment you like, check it over, are there any visible defects?

Yes / **No**

Yes → Are you willing/is it possible to fix this?

No → If there are pockets or buttons, are they functioning (not faux)?

Are you willing/is it possible to fix this?
- **Yes** → Is this one of your only options?
- **No** → If you were looking for a sign, don't buy it.

Is this one of your only options?
- **Yes** → Check the composition label, is there synthetic fibre used?
- **No** → I think we should find a better one!

If there are pockets or buttons, are they functioning (not faux)?
- **Yes** → Look at the inside of the garment, is it as nice on the inside as it is on the outside?
- **No** → Reconsider purchasing this, especially if it's stretching your budget. Functioning buttons and pockets are a basic element of garments.

Look at the inside of the garment, is it as nice on the inside as it is on the outside?
- **Yes**
- **No** → This may not be worth the £££

Check the composition label, is there synthetic fibre used? → **Yes**

Is there synthetic fibre used?
- **Yes** → Does this piece have a point of view? For example, is the design totally unique or is it a vintage?
- **No** → Repair is an essential part of shopping responsibly, this is a garment we can consider.

Wardrobe Audit

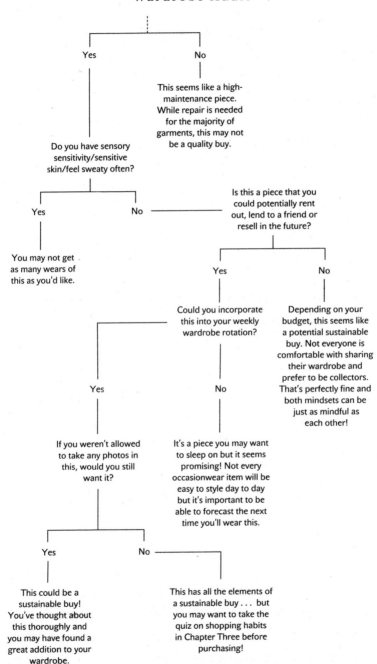

Yes

No

This seems like a high-maintenance piece. While repair is needed for the majority of garments, this may not be a quality buy.

Do you have sensory sensitivity/sensitive skin/feel sweaty often?

Is this a piece that you could potentially rent out, lend to a friend or resell in the future?

Yes

No

You may not get as many wears of this as you'd like.

Yes

No

Could you incorporate this into your weekly wardrobe rotation?

Depending on your budget, this seems like a potential sustainable buy. Not everyone is comfortable with sharing their wardrobe and prefer to be collectors. That's perfectly fine and both mindsets can be just as mindful as each other!

Yes

No

If you weren't allowed to take any photos in this, would you still want it?

It's a piece you may want to sleep on but it seems promising! Not every occasionwear item will be easy to style day to day but it's important to be able to forecast the next time you'll wear this.

Yes

No

This could be a sustainable buy! You've thought about this thoroughly and you may have found a great addition to your wardrobe.

This has all the elements of a sustainable buy . . . but you may want to take the quiz on shopping habits in Chapter Three before purchasing!

Summary

✦ No one is immune from feeling like they have nothing to wear.

✦ A capsule wardrobe differs for everyone, so don't buy into the idea that everyone needs the same 'staples'.

✦ Shopping isn't reductive; we cannot put a perfect number on the amount of items you should have.

✦ Learning to 'shop' from your wardrobe can provide the same excitement as buying something new.

✦ Understanding what you dislike and why in your wardrobe is more important than looking at what you do.

✦ A wardrobe audit is essential every season to remind yourself of your needs and makes getting dressed easier.

Chapter 2

MONEY
&
MENTAL HEALTH

✦

If you've gotten this far you probably think, 'Damn, this girl has a lot of problems.' My therapists agree with you.

A significant part of my adult life has been spent living with imposter syndrome. Throughout my teens and twenties, I absolutely dreaded celebrations. The idea of applauding 'me' would make my skin prickle with dread. Frankly, it's because I thought I didn't deserve it. This thought has followed me throughout my career. At the height of my imposter syndrome, I received a nomination as Best Fashion Influencer 2019 but ended up leaving an hour into the award ceremony. Even staying as long as that had me on the edge of a panic attack. It made me sick to the stomach being in that room. I believed that everyone else deserved their recognition so much more and I was an anomaly who shouldn't even have been invited.

There are many reasons why I felt this way. Lots of them are things I can't control, like being an ethnic minority in a predominantly white fashion industry, but there was a big factor that I could work on that helped me a lot – reconciling an internal divide. Like I mentioned before, a part of me wanted the status, the fancy trips and beautiful gifts that saturate the social media and fashion industry. The other part wanted to be rid of all the nonsense. I just wanted to do a job where I could uncover the wonderful parts of fashion – the creative, collaborative side that uplifts and inspires people.

Being torn is confusing and frustrating enough. It also makes it hard to progress in life and contributes to that awful feeling of stagnation. But what caused more suffering was living with this internal divide for so many years. And it resulted in a career and a life that I was deeply dissatisfied with.

This chapter is about money and mental health, which is at the heart of the five steps. We talk a lot about living according to our values and how this is the route to inner peace. But there's just not enough emphasis on the benefits of starting with how and where you put your money. As always, the Mindful Monday Method is not here to categorise anyone or anything into 'good', 'bad' or 'could do better'. It's about providing you with the tools to make important decisions for yourself.

We'll go through reflection and journaling exercises to explore any money-related habits that have affected your wellbeing. As I lead you through the thought processes that helped me and formed the backbone of the Mindful Monday Method, I'm also going to introduce you to Dr Dion Terrelonge, a fashion psychologist. When I asked her what tip she can give people who want to shop better for their mental health, 'intention' is the word that she came up with: 'Examining your motivations for why you're going shopping is a first step and even writing them down because this will help you to be more conscious of what you're doing.'

I can't tell you what to do. I can't dictate which brands you should wear or when or where to buy things. It doesn't help anyone to transfer control from brands over to me. This is your chance to regain control.

Put your money where your mind is

Open your mobile banking app, look at your statements or take a look at whatever you use to track your spending. What takes the biggest chunk out of your account? Things like bills, rent and groceries are generally considered to be essentials. We'll instead be looking at the indulgences. The little 'pop-ins' to shops on your lunch break. The pick-me-up treats that catch your eye on your walk home. These don't have to stop entirely, only until you have a firm grasp on your wealth wellness. Let's recalibrate some of the most common toxic habits we've cultivated because, as a society, we aren't just consumerists: we're excessively so.

Task

'Where your treasure is, there your heart will be also.'

This quote inspired me to think about how our finances can reveal our innermost desires. It can be applied to the idea that we spend most of our disposable income on what we value. It may seem obvious to some but for others who experience a disconnect between who we think we should be versus who we want to be, it's a very revealing exercise.

There is only a concern to address if the results make you feel uncomfortable. For example, as an adult (and the jury is out as to whether this is cool or not), I started collecting Sylvanian Family toys. Yes, those cartoonish miniature animals that live in dolls houses. There were a few months where my expenditure on this was considerable, but I have no regrets and could afford it.

Take into account your top three categories with the highest spend in the last three months and write them down here:

1. Highest spend:

Why:

Length of time (How long has it been in the top three?):

2.

Why:

Length of time:

3.

Why:

Length of time:

This is an exercise to help you to start a habit of thinking a certain way, so you can choose what you want to reflect on and figure out what truly motivates your spending. Write down what prompted your decision to spend the money in the 'why' section. I would start with something palatable but significant, like an addiction to a certain car sharing app . . .

I'm prone to anxiety, especially in crowds. This is something that's hard to avoid if you take public transport. In the years 2020 to 2022, my expenditure on private transport skyrocketed. It wasn't because I was being snooty, refusing to sit on gum-covered seats in a rickety carriage, shuttling deep below the streets of London. My unwanted habit was influenced by the racist incidents I experienced during this time. Going out made me feel incredibly unsafe. So for that period, while I was trying to build up the courage to live, work and socialise in a city I've called my home for the majority of my life, it was entirely worth it to pay a premium in travel. But it also wasn't sustainable (in all senses of the word) long term. I'm glad to say that my relationship with that ride app is at more of an acquaintance level now. But the moral of the story is that it's OK to extend compassion to yourself, even with indulgences.

If you're interested in how I broke that habit, I found a coping mechanism that I think can be applied to shopping too. I made a point of looking back on the day before and saying to myself, 'Nothing bad happened.' If it helps you to see it and write it, you can even mark it on a calendar. Soon enough, I had seven whole days where I didn't have any negative experiences when I was out in public.

After a few more weeks of this, I could travel without

thinking too much about those hypothetical, threatening scenarios that used to run rampant in my mind. If anything negative were to happen, I knew that statistically this was an anomaly.

For many, when it comes to spending too much. Naturally, we want to do things that make us feel better. Shopping is often like a Happy Meal, where the anticipation of the toy outweighs the taste of the food. However, once we've ripped open the cute, bright little paper lunchbox and played with the tiny plastic accompaniment for ten minutes, we would never be seen with it again.

If you struggle with spending more than you'd like, the fact you're even aware of it is a great first step. Can I recommend a process of building up a series of days where you don't buy anything on a whim and marking it on a calendar? I bet at the very least the restraint will make you feel the same or better in mood – but definitely not worse. One of the biggest challenges here is the *fear* of feeling worse than the original reason why we feel bad. But when money is involved, I struggle to think of an example outside of paying for therapy where spending truly has a long-term positive net effect. Try it for a week, then push yourself for two. Perhaps this is the little bit of encouragement you need to start replacing cheeky impulse buys or expensive coffees with something else.

Mark this calendar to practise keeping track

1	2	3
4	5	6
7	8	9
10	11	12
13	14	15
16	17	18
19	20	21
22	23	24
25	26	27
28	29	30
31		

To make this exercise more effective, you can switch your motivation to spend. Instead, start planning experience-based dopamine hits that are equal to or less than your usual output. For example, if we take the £300 that some-one called Zara seems to leech from your bank account every month, this can easily score a weekend trip to a new city or even a staycation on your own. Or what about a nice meal out or a night in with friends? Whatever floats your boat and transfers dependency on physical fashion items (which you'll realise is quite hard to get rid of from the wardrobe audit) to more meaningful activities that encourage connection with friends and even nature.

Coming back to our reflection, I'd like to discuss two other points. First, you may feel that there's no need to stop spending a lot. On my way home one evening, I found myself making small talk with a friend's friend. If you ever want succinct answers, the escalator of an underground station is a great place for that. As the mechanical steps descended into the fluorescent lighting of the concourse and crowds flock towards their platforms, he asked, 'What do you do?'

'I teach people how to shop better for their mental health and the planet. I believe that if people really knew how to do this, they wouldn't want to spend as much as they do now,' I said.

He responded with, 'I buy too many things that I don't really need or want but I don't want to stop spending.'

It then occurred to me that in certain cultures,

the idea of admitting that you'd like to limit your expenditure is somewhat of an attack on the ego. I would like to highlight that this want (or need) has no bearing on income level. In Business of Fashion's annual report, State of Fashion (2023), findings revealed that an overwhelming majority of shoppers in the US aged 18–65+ were proactively seeking lower-priced fashion. The most interesting takeaway is that while Gen Z and Millennials were the most interested in this (87 per cent and 81 per cent respectively), when it comes to income levels, there was a mere 3 per cent difference between low income and high income.[xi] This suggests that everyone, no matter how much disposable income they have, is reconsidering price when it comes to fashion. Everyone can benefit from having an extra bit of cash. There will always be a better place to put it than in your wardrobe.

The second point is important because everything is made that little bit more achievable when there's a time limit. Take a look at your vampiric category, the one that you view as a money pit. When it comes to determining the length of time for these large expenditures, we're looking at whether it's a one-off situation, a recurring but recent spend that's exclusive to those three months or likely to be long term. Time can help to expose the severity of the issue and I'm not talking about debt because that's definitely for a financial expert. I'm talking about easing a bad shopping habit that's been taking a toll on your finances for a while.

For me, when I finally faced up to the fact that taxis were leaving a massive dent in my account, I wanted that money pit to be filled with cement immediately. Perhaps even lay a nice roll of fresh turf over it and pretend it never happened. For that expenditure to be reduced and stay low long term, I had to decide if this was circumstantial or something that I would rely on in the future. Remember, this is incredibly personal so you may need differing amounts of time. In any case, have an idea of how long you can afford to keep it up, emotionally and fiscally speaking.

In my case, building up courage to interact with strangers and travel with crowds at peak times took about two months. I might alternate: for example, if I took a taxi to a location I would walk or take public transport back. Never twice in the same day. When I could handle that, I started avoiding taking taxis two days in a row. Then three and so on, until I did it only when it was strictly necessary. It helps to put a time or condition on this too: for example, if I am travelling home after 10pm and I'm alone.

It can be applied to your area of overspending. Let's take a common example, which is more merchant based. If your money pit happens to be Amazon, consider cancelling your Prime membership. Inserting a barrier isn't depriving yourself but making you think twice about hitting 'check out'. None of us like the idea of paying for shipping but in case you didn't realise, none of it is actually free. Someone or something somewhere is bearing the cost. So while it may feel like a nuisance shelling out a few more quid to get something delivered, remember that it could make your purchases more considered. Don't look at it as a like for like: a membership fee for free shipping and convenience versus £5.99 every time you want a top up of loo roll. You could potentially save more in the long run because, let's be honest, often we're buying a bunch of random things along with that 12-pack of toilet paper.

Next, adapt your length of time to a weekly shop to coincide with your groceries. If you're in the mindset of buying apples and bread, you'll be focused more on the essentials instead of browsing for a moisturiser that promises to be delivered tomorrow by 7pm.

I hope that gives you inspiration for how you might be able to place boundaries with your spending and create context around each of those categories.

At this point, I'd like to introduce the concept of paying yourself. This is what's really going to help make these habits stick because it makes all of it very worthwhile. Now, paying yourself isn't an original, genius idea that I came up with. Admittedly, I can't tell you who did. I think it's one of those things that has always existed.

The thought came to me when I was scrolling on social media. I saw a snippet of a video where a woman said something like, 'You are the same person no matter how much money you have, so if you don't start saving when you have £100, you won't when you have £100,000.' If you said that and you're reading this, I'm sorry if I've messed up your quote. However, it really inspired me to think about 'Future Me'.

There are some things that Future Me is likely to do and will be 100 per cent fine with it. Like it's highly probable that Future Me is also going to want dessert and to stay for another drink, OK? But she won't be impressed if in the present, I buy a tiny handbag that's only large enough for my self-esteem and a tampon.

So every time you think, 'Ah! I want a new pair of cashmere bed socks', ask: would I rather pay myself the amount that that costs? More times than not, we'd rather take the cash and run.

It helps to keep a diary of all the things you resisted (it also helps with putting your money where your mind is!) and at the end of the week or month, add it up. You can even add the amount it would have cost you to your calendar, where you've also marked each day that passed without an impulse buy. At the end of the week, I strongly suggest that you transfer that amount to another account so that you can see it accumulate. It's the most satisfying thing to do and adds up very quickly. If you don't have a spare account, you can consider withdrawing it in cash and keeping it somewhere safe. Or sending it to someone you trust, like your spouse or parent, and treat it like a holiday or gift fund. The effectiveness of this exercise is centred around visualising and benefitting from consistent good spending choices. It's about shifting your mindset from cheap thrills to longer-term, more meaningful investments.

You may worry about having less to spend if you're constantly transferring the cost of little luxuries out of your main account. But the thing is, you're still keeping those funds. They're just separate and a little more out of reach. The alternative would've been to squander it and you would still feel stretched. The result of paying yourself is a nice nest egg to invest in something you truly want.

And if your goal is to simply start saving, you can use this exercise as a way to build up an emergency fund. Combining paying yourself with the previous exercise that analysed what and why we were spending so much of our disposable income, we are practicing something called habit stacking. This is the accumulation of positive practices that help to entrench desired behaviours that become long-term practices. When you get to the stage where you feel less burdened by unnecessary purchases and a leaky bank account, I don't promise you happiness, but I'm certain you'll have more peace of mind.

Money and childhood experiences

The first uncomfortable question we're going to address is 'how old do you feel when you're stressed about money?'

I feel 15 and not in a Taylor Swift kind of way.

My birthday always falls around Chinese New Year. This date follows the lunar calendar and therefore, it changes annually. The tradition of receiving red packets full of money from relatives and family friends is for all unmarried people, but youths benefit most from this. For me, thanks to the double celebration, I usually received twice the cash. However, once you're past the age of 21, the level of generosity from Asian elders isn't quite the same. Somehow, their enthusiasm wanes once they're giving money to someone who's old enough to shave their legs and buy alcohol. But throughout my early teens, when I appreciated what a wad of £20 notes could do, it was one of the few times that I felt acknowledged. It's worth noting that I didn't receive money just for being older. There's a lot of ceremony and performance that goes into obtaining those envelopes.

The connection between having resources to spend and feeling secure and loved was reinforced every time I received an award or got good grades at school. I was a junior athlete in the Olympics of affection and I frequently won gold. As a teenager wandering around shopping malls in north London, I was confident that my intelligence (which I soon discovered was completely relative to my environment) would quickly recuperate what I spent. My shopping was frantic. I'd rush from store to store like a real-life version of Diner Dash to collect as many tokens of love as my coins could afford.

At 15, this was the first time in my life I experienced the frenzy of having to work to catch up with my spending habits. As I progressed to more high-achieving schools, it became harder to get the grades and the pocket prize money that came with it. By the time I finished my A levels, I never clawed back all that I had squandered on high street clothing. Through this, another toxic association was formed: self-worth is tied to how much you have.

The pursuit and maintenance of status has so quickly become one of society's greatest evils yet it's so commonly mistaken as a blessing. For people of colour, especially first and second generation immigrants, this comes as an expression of acculturative stress. As we try to assimilate, there's an overwhelming pressure to 'prove ourselves' and the pursuit of status becomes an effective tool to gain social acceptance. It's our survival instinct and, consciously or not, this is taught to children.

At first, the plan makes a lot of sense. Get yourself a high level of education so that you can work a well-salaried job. Earn enough and perhaps you can avoid the traumas that your parents experienced. But the flipside is that we might grow up learning to self-soothe with shiny bags. We display them like trophies on shelves while we chase new accolades. The old ones collect dust as they go out of season, but we continue to replenish our emptying well of self-care with more emblems of success. More logos, more 'it' products, more money thrown to the wind. And on it goes, until we not only devalue the items we bought, but we also diminish our worth to a line-up of designer *things*.

Vicky Reynal is a financial psychotherapist specialising in people's relationship with money and helps clients understand their emotional triggers when overspending or overcoming financial trauma. In her book, *Money on Your Mind,* she writes, 'We don't all have the same relationship with money, and to understand our attitude towards it we have to dig into our past experiences for information about what it might stand for in our lives,' which is why one of the most important exercises in curbing our unwanted thirst for consumption lies in exploring the beginning of those coping mechanisms – the little versions of ourselves.

Task: How old do you feel when you're stressed about money?

Use the space at the end of the book as a place to journal your thoughts. There is no perfectionism in streams of consciousness. Simply write what comes to mind and try to fill the page. Use additional pages of paper if needed.

Do you remember the concept of Future Me? Whenever I want to admonish myself for a foolish spending spree or an extravagant purchase I didn't plan for, I picture myself ten years from now as a stable (emotionally and fiscally) individual. What would she say to me?

I used the same technique on a friend who had recently graduated from university. She shared how worried she was about the cost of living and how she felt guilty even going out to eat, or using air conditioning in a heatwave. But those restrictive behaviours didn't actually comfort her; they made her want to compulsively shop all the more.

'What would Future You say about how you're handling your finances now?' I asked her.

'That I'm allowed to live my life, just don't be stupid,' was the response. Prior to that question, she had expressed paragraphs of negative thoughts where she had begun spiralling into anxiety. That succinct, clear and self-compassionate answer was a step forward in reframing her fear around money.

If we visualise our present selves as younger and in need of reassurance, not criticism, it's far easier to be kind. It's helpful to do this when you want to break that awful, suffocating sensation that comes with catastrophising. The thing with anxiety is that it takes a grain of truth (for example, that we don't have a lot) and builds entire scenarios out of this. Sometimes, if you have a wild imagination like I do, there's enough content there for Marvel to create an entire multiverse. And this is exactly how we create warped perceptions of reality that are just as fantastical as sci-fi movies. Fear stifles our senses and confuses our reasoning, until we no longer live in the present world. Instead, we exist in a nightmarish version of it that retains just enough realism to convince us that we need to stay and fight our way out through more overthinking, more worrying. And we do this because it gives us that control we so crave over our spending habits.

It's not our fault, or our parents' fault, or even our grandparents' fault that we struggle with overspending. Our caretakers or parents modelled what role money plays in our lives but most do so unconsciously. Vicky gives the example of 'growing up in poverty, absorbing our parents' anxieties about its insufficiency, or watching them be critical of money as something that "spoils" people'. The idea of spending more than a certain amount on a single garment feels daunting to some, even if they're considered high earners. 'Did we receive our first money unconditionally (like a weekly allowance) or was it linked to achievements or good behaviour? The sum of all the experiences we picked up unconsciously growing up, from our family environment as well as the society we grew up in, will have shaped our view of money and our behaviour with it.' The worst thing we can do is add self-judgement and shame to the mix. Once we're able to show some grace towards ourselves, it's remarkable how much clarity and peace can come with it.

We are not what we wear

If you want to shop, you're not the problem.
If you want to buy new, you're not the problem.
If you want to look good, you're not the problem.

One of the greatest challenges in working in the sustainable fashion space is the language we use. So often it's in binaries or absolutes: 'Just don't shop fast fashion' or 'How can you say you care about the environment if you're still doing [insert behaviour here]?'. If you've ever experienced anything like the above, I can tell you that, again, you're not the problem. The problem with the kind of people that behave like this who also claim to be sustainability activists is that they're closer to those street preachers yelling that we're all going to hell than they are do-gooders.

More than that, I've always wondered why the conversation about 'irresponsible shopping' seems to be so gendered, the onus almost always being placed on women. Dr Terrelonge believes that as infants, women are 'taught to prioritise how we look and in particular, how we look to others', as this becomes the basis of affirmation of our character and something that we internalise. On the other hand, men aren't exposed to the same vocabulary. 'They're told from a young age, "Oh, aren't they rambunctious? Aren't they so smart? Aren't they creative?" They get feedback that is more about their internal states and who they are and their skills,' she adds.

So if women are more likely to view their aesthetic preferences as an extension of who they really are, we are also far more susceptible to taking fashion incredibly personally. As if we really are what we wear. I'm here to tell you that there is nothing wrong with buying something we *want* but know that we don't need. The only problem with that picture is that so often we forget that objects are there to serve our needs, not the other way around. When things aren't in the right order, you'll find that we start to build our identity on very shaky ground: on the crumbling pedestals of brand association and aspirational but out-of-reach lifestyles.

An example of this might be an individual that prides themselves on having an impressive collection of shoes. They're always in the know about design collaborations, which retailer has exclusive designs and spends the majority of their disposable income on this collection. These factors in themselves aren't a problem, they're an interest and a pretty cool one at that. The point where that person stops wearing the shoes and the shoes begin to wear them is when their identity and self-worth is tied to the ownership of these things. Instead of using fashion to articulate ourselves, we become walking advertisements for an array of brands and tell ourselves that 'those who get it, get it and those that don't, don't'.

Dr Terrelonge tells me that one of the healthy ways individuals can relate to fashion and their personal style is if 'they're able to use clothing confidently to reflect who they are. They're not trying to dress for other people and they're looking internally at themselves rather than externally', thereby viewing themselves not through the lens of another but through understanding who they are.

Take a look at the exercise below and reconnect with who you are.

Aligning self-love and your image

Task

Write down three things that you value about yourself that aren't based on physical attributes:

1.

2.

3.

Write down three things that fashion makes you feel emotionally. Some of these prompts may help:

When browsing garments online, are you mindlessly scrolling or do you feel present? What is the root of the emotion you feel as you do this?

When you look through your social media feed at fashionable individuals are you aware of your emotions? If so, what are they?

When you're trying on clothes, what's going through your mind?

1.

2.

3.

I'll bet you those two sets of answers didn't overlap. It isn't that surprising that being our best selves isn't supported by our current models of fashion. When I asked my online audience to do this task, I discovered some interesting things. Very few people wanted to tell me three things that they valued about themselves, but I got far more responses when I asked them how clothes made them feel, which is arguably a more sensitive question.

Ultimately, fashion makes people feel conflicted. So

many respondents said it makes them feel 'confident' but also 'not good enough', 'too big/short' and 'unattractive'. This reminds me of the previous chapter – the quiz to discover why we have nothing to wear. As one respondent put it, fashion makes us feel 'not quite right'.

Before I started my journey with sustainable fashion and established the Mindful Monday Method, I couldn't even tell you three things I valued about myself. Old me would probably have given you a superficial answer, like how I value that my hair is always shiny. It was a way to avoid acknowledging that I really had no sense of self.

Now I can tell you that the three traits I like about myself are that I'm compassionate, creative and self-aware. And I can now say that my shopping choices reflect this. Being able to identify three characteristics that you admire about yourself is also going to be helpful in Chapter Three, when we'll discuss how to align your best self with how and where you choose to shop.

However, in previous years, the best version of myself was very much hindered by my shopping choices. Fashion used to make me feel inadequate. It made me feel lonely. I'd think, 'If clothes are meant to make you part of a tribe, where's mine? Why can't I see my taste reflected in what's popular online?' Worse than feeling like an outsider, fashion made me feel out of control. So much of the problem comes down to how we separate our purchase decisions from the rest of our actions. I'm not making this into a moral or even an ethical point; I'm highlighting the need to reconcile the major discrepancies in our lives, at least the ones we have control over, in order to be at peace.

Remember how I said that you're not the problem? Well, I'll tell you what is: the idea that we have no way out of the mess that the fashion industry has accumulated through wilful ignorance. But there is an exit. Saying no to one bad garment at a time, rooted in the belief that it's a choice as to whether we want our clothes to define us. We can check the care labels all we want. We can resist the siren call of Zara, avoid the temptation of Mango and flee from the doorstep of H&M. But if we don't confront the truth that we are *not* what we wear, we will eventually succumb to the clever false promises of a snake-print knee-high boot.

The psychology of retail

My first full time job out of university was at a retail store as an assistant manager. I was 21 years old and knew that I wanted to work in fashion but couldn't find any other way in. I walked through the doors of the three storey flagship with very little expectations, bar banking a pay cheque. When I emerged a year later on antidepressants and six kilograms lighter (and also in need of prescription opticals), I had seen first hand what effective retail psychology looked like. I didn't expect to take away so much understanding of its effectiveness. As the universal 'they' say, everything happens for a reason. Perhaps the reason for one of the toughest jobs I ever had to do is so

I could tell you all about how physical shops are set up to optimise sales.

Sensory branding was key. All of its stores around the world at the retail chain I worked for, no matter if it was in a mall in the middle of a small US state or a towering landmark building in an Asian city, faithfully pumped its iconic fragrance through the ventilation system. The same tracks played at a set volume, never to be tampered with, no matter how many parents complained about the noise as they waited for their teenagers to pick out another logo t-shirt. You wanted to touch everything – fabrics were always soft, distressed and exuded nonchalant wealth. But the visuals are what people always remember. Although, ironically, you couldn't see very much with how dim the lighting was. Tables, fitted displays and rails were moved or rebuilt to optimise whatever garment it housed. This was important to ensure that garments never grazed the floor – that was too mass market, this was 'accessible luxury'. I remember climbing an enormous ladder – that I recall as being at least two storeys high – with a protractor in hand just to measure the angle of the enormous overhead light so it would hit the mural of half-naked men in sports gear *just right*. Honestly, to this day, I'm still unsure if that was even necessary or if my manager was having a bad day and thought it would be funny to see me squirm. Nevertheless, brand senses were everything.

We can't forget about the models. Dancing on the balconies, topless at the door with brilliant white teeth or folding the same cable knit over and over again . . . the sales assistants were the centre of attention. They were zoned across the shop floor according to how well they fitted the 'look' of the brand. It goes without saying, this was fucked up. But something more uncomfortable should be addressed – the fact that this worked so incredibly well at selling an aspirational lifestyle to anyone aged 13–32. Even though my perception of Gen Z (those born between 1997 and 2012) is that they're far more self-aware, and accepting of differences than my generation, this concept still works in popularising brands today.

There are still global and thriving fashion retailers that are staffed in the main, by young, attractive women and it's interesting because brands like these tend to sell to Gen Z. The very demographic you might expect to reject such archaic notions of Eurocentric, thin beauty.

These are some basic examples in retail psychology around what you can see, smell, hear and even touch but so much more goes into designing the ideal retail space. Paolo de Cesare is a fashion CEO with some of the most recognisable multi-brand retailer names under his belt. Ever heard of the iconic Parisian luxury department store Printemps? Or perhaps you have browsed for a handbag on Matches Fashion? If anyone knows anything about how to sell fashion, it's him. When it comes to designing the perfect store, cynics may think that it's all about playing games with our minds, using nefarious selling tactics or even trying to use AI. But if that were the whole truth, wouldn't that put us off shopping?

Why Don't I Have Anything to Wear?

Let's leave fashion for a moment and think about how you feel when you shop at IKEA, an example that de Cesare gives as a 'standard of excellence for creating very coherent categories'. Ignore the potential arguments with your flatmate or the dread of actually having to put flatpack furniture together and focus on the actual experience of wandering around the mocked-up rooms, with their corresponding products. 'It's a different market of course, but you'll have a bathroom, the kitchen, the living room, the bedroom – they are super clear. You have everything you need in this universe, in the same area. And they are put in sequential order in a way that you can navigate it very easily.' I have a friend that actually suggests to potential dates that they should go to IKEA because it's such an easy place to hang out. It's also worth noting that when you go to the Scandi homeware haven, the only thing you tend to regret buying is the extra plate of meatballs with lingonberry sauce. And even then, can you really be that mad at yourself? One of the largest factors in creating a space that reduces stress for the shopper is simplicity. Just make it make sense. That seems to be a pretty great brief for anyone doing the layout of a store, but not quite.

When it comes to creating the perfect department store, you can't win at everything. Harrods is at the top of the physical retail game. But let's be honest, even if you had to have the means to shop there, it's not an easy place to do so. Go in one of the many entrances and you're faced with a maze of luxury timepieces and jewellery houses, but come from the other end and it's a plethora of brightly lit beauty concessions. There's even a set of doors that leads directly into an endless corridor of designer bags and one that opens to an escalator system. So there's a reason that no matter who you ask on the shop floor, they know exactly where each department is and can succinctly tell you how to find it. They're the London black cab drivers of the retail world. Harrods was founded in 1849 and has built a reputation for being able to service any client with any request – even exotic animals, at least up until the late 1970s. For the year 2021/2022, after a series of lockdowns in the UK, Harrods reportedly took in £652.4 million,[xii] nearly a 35 per cent increase from last year. In comparison, the much smaller and quaint store Liberty reportedly turned over £82 million.[xiii] It's that crucial point that they don't just house destination items but the act of visiting the store itself is the destination. This sets them apart in spite of being a tricky department store to navigate.

For other physical retail spaces that don't have the prestige of being an icon in itself, De Cesare says, 'You have traffic and destination categories. A traffic category is one where people browse through and can purchase by impulse. A destination is one where people will go to even the fiftieth floor to find that item.' Depending on the culture and changing demands of customers, these categories may change. De Cesare gives shoes as an example of one that was previously a destination and is now a traffic driver, citing the US as a region where shoppers may more commonly find them on the ground floor. However, a few divisions that don't tend to leave this prime space and continue to drive quick purchases are accessibly priced jewellery brands and beauty counters.

Department stores are also heavily gendered. And as much as we don't like to talk in binaries and of course men wear perfume and makeup too, these spaces are very much geared towards selling to women. There's a question that we can potentially ask ourselves: how much of our shopping habits are formed by societal conditioning?

Alec Leach, the author of *The World Is On Fire But We're Still Buying Shoes*, shares my sentiment that 'menswear is generally thought of as less disposable as womenswear', although in recent years the industries are sharing more similarities. It's precisely because menswear has previously been less trend-led that one of the tips I give to people who are looking to find better-quality basics is to look in the menswear department. Genderless things like t-shirts, loungewear and athleisure items such as hoodies and knitwear have consistently reviewed better. Shirts use heavier weights for cotton, meaning that they're not as sheer and they're softer. There's less synthetic where it doesn't need to be. A large factor that influences this is that men's clothing tends to prioritise classic tailoring over microtrends. The focus is more on fit, everyday styling and providing clothes that last. Wait, let me elaborate on that. Clothes that last that don't require a ton of polyester. If the menswear department can do that, why can't womenswear? This is where I think things start to become a little too much like mind games. The thing is, retailers can but it's not a lucrative thing to do. I've asked menswear designers and the men themselves what their biggest reasons for returning clothes are. Often it's the quality of fit and, second to that, if their partner detests it. Hands up, who here has made their significant other return a hideous shirt?

On the topic of returns, men don't tend to do this as much as women. And it's not because the ladies are indecisive. The fashion industry kind of sets us up for inconvenience. If you've ever noticed, men's sizing actually follows measurements. For example, when looking at a pair of trousers, men might see a 30 waist with a 32 inseam (the length from crotch to ankle). They'll know whether or not that fits. Then descriptors like 'regular', 'tapered' or 'slim' indicate what the silhouette will be. It's also far easier to buy a shirt when it's measured by neck size in inches and the shopper knows that the standard sleeve length is 32–33 inches. In 1868, the first ready-to-wear collection was menswear and introduced by the Belgian Dewatcher Brothers. A lot of the ability to provide this for men first was that the shape the male form isn't as variable. From that point of view, it's simpler for brands to cater to men through this form of size labelling.

However, it doesn't quite explain other discrepancies. Like how premium menswear outfitters often provide complimentary tailoring but womenswear brands don't. And arguably, the most frustrating of all: the plague of vanity sizing. Have you noticed how different brands seem to have varying measurements for the same nominal size (hence the demand for AI fit advisors, as discussed in Chapter One)? Vanity sizing is a problem that exists mostly in womenswear. It's also known as size inflation, which is when the same size (for example, UK 14) remains the same on the label but over time, increases in its measurements. The intention is to make the wearer feel that they're wearing the same size even if they're not. It's supposed to be flattering, hence the 'vanity' part of the term. In reality, I feel that it only reinforces the idea that we should be very pleased with ourselves if our weight doesn't fluctuate. There's a huge degree of psychology in fashion and the gender biases are astonishing.

Shopping should be an enjoyable experience and it's easy to forget that when we're inundated with poor-quality items that don't quite match their asking prices or when we're thinking about the amount of new clothes and its impact on the environment. Retailers are optimising store experiences to reduce the friction to purchase and at best, this can be an inspiring trip. At worst – well we know the feeling of coming home from the shops, battered and bruised from an impossible quest. However, knowledge is key and understanding the industry will only help you make better decisions. If we are to be realistic – as I believe good purchase decisions need to take place in our reality and not in a hypothetical construct – we will continue to shop. So how we feel as we're doing so is highly important.

To shop mindfully, we need to prioritise experiences that leave us feeling good. After all, it's not as if the majority of us have the very noble grand plan to stop buying anything forever.

Unlearning toxic shopping habits

There are a few beliefs that really stand out to me because every time I mention them, people respond with 'How did you know I do that?!' or 'I feel seen'. One common mindset that shoppers have is when they look for an imaginary item that doesn't exist. I like to think the most creative among us do this – you think about a particular piece of clothing in a specific colour or print or silhouette. You absolutely cannot attend that event or begin your first day at work without wearing it. And so you embark on a wild goose chase which leaves you frustrated.

Then there's the habit of shopping when you're bored. So much of the time, we're unconsciously scrolling, looking for inspiration. For compulsive shoppers, it's almost second to breathing. We find ourselves on page three of what's 'New In' on our favourite e-commerce site every time we're on our phone having downtime.

But shopping is not entertainment, despite the way that it's been sold to us. If you've ever thought to yourself, 'I don't want to do this anymore' but you're unable to stop, Dr Dion calls it as she sees it: compulsive shopping. 'It's almost out of your hands. And when it's compulsive, you're not in control anymore. And that's when it starts becoming about your mental health.'

If you do shop compulsively or because you are bored, you're not alone and many, including me, have been able to overcome this by having a set of filters in place (that we will learn together) that stop us from buying things unnecessarily. Every day, I get the most amazing inspirational messages from the Mindful Monday community. One I'd like to share with you read, 'A note of gratitude: You have managed to destroy my impulsive shopping habit. I have learnt a lot from you and my wardrobe has become more sustainable'.

Now is the time to address something that isn't on the checklist overleaf but is a common pitfall. A good friend of mine has a strong sense of personal style. She often jokes that it's based on the same three colours that happen to be neutrals: beige, white and black. Sometimes grey if she's feeling spicy. She showed me her Pinterest board full of outfit inspiration, exclaiming, 'I wish I could dress like that!' I glanced at her cream linen ensemble and her chic 1990s-style shoulder bag – she looked exactly like what was on her moodboard.

I hope she forgives me for using her as an example. I've come across this dissonance multiple times but she sticks out to me so much because she's well dressed with an identifiable style. When someone already presents the ideal aesthetic they want yet is dissatisfied, Dr Dion says, 'There may be something about what that style embodies that they feel they're not yet embodying.'

To which I responded, 'You look the part but you don't feel the part.' I think a lot of us can relate to that. It's part of why I hate the common saying in fashion (and many other industries): 'Fake it till you make it'. It's clear that while clothing can temporarily imbue us with a sense of confidence, if we're not careful it also becomes a crutch that doesn't quite solve the problem, which lies within. So if we do happen to 'make it', we have the sense that our wardrobes are a few steps ahead of us.

Over the last few years, from my own experience and my community, I've uncovered the most common 'toxic shopping habits'. A combination of these show that we might be subservient to material objects and we may even be at risk of losing control of our finances. Take a look at the most common ones I've encountered and tick off any of those that apply to you.

- ☐ You hate being photographed in a repeat outfit.
- ☐ Your social media feed is mainly hauls.
- ☐ You spend more than you're comfortable with on fashion.
- ☐ You have a wish-list you're always updating.
- ☐ When you shop you try to find imaginary items you've made up.
- ☐ You buy clothes that aren't your size and hope you can 'make it work'.
- ☐ You buy into trends because you convince yourself they'll come back in fashion eventually.

☐ You have clothes with tags on that are past the refund date.

☐ You buy things primarily because they seem like a good deal.

☐ You find yourself browsing when you're stressed or bored.

☐ You make up an entire life-changing story based on buying one garment.

☐ You'll sacrifice all else for 'aesthetics'.

How to tackle toxic shopping habits

Clothing within your means

I asked my audience if social media platforms encouraged them to spend beyond their limits. Seventy-five per cent said they believe it to be the main source of temptation. Parallel to this, I may be known as the creator that's more likely to proclaim that [insert brand's collection here] 'isn't worth it' more than say it is – all based on analysis from the Mindful Monday Method – yet I am constantly asked to provide links to things to buy. I'm not opposed to this request. If someone wants to shop, I would rather they bought something with a low risk of planned obsolescence and a lesser impact to the environment, and I am here to direct people to those things. But I think there's a more important message that comes before recommendations.

Most people may believe that polished street style photos and fashion videos convince them that they should buy something they weren't planning to. However, 13 per cent from the same poll also admitted that if not social media, it would be something else encouraging them to shop.

Dr Helen Powell is an associate professor in creative advertising at London's Southbank University. She argues that one of the reasons we constantly seek new clothes is because we have learnt to 'see ourselves photo-graphically', through representing ourselves to others on social media apps. We are constantly thirsting to communicate who we are and our social relevance through our taste and choices.

Moreover, we might find ourselves caught in this internal conflict of wanting to do what's best for our mental health and wallets – which is to resist spending too much – and the constant need for reinvention, which fashion allows. If this sounds like you, here's one tactic that's helped me: clothing within your means. This is an approach that looks at one of the most practical aspects of fashion – your literal wardrobe space. If you don't have the means to house your garments (without buying a storage unit a 15-minute drive away), then it's possible that you may need to rethink the amount that you have.

Through wardrobe audits, I've been able to reclaim a substantial area that seasonal fashion had colonised. (Storing winter coats in vacuum bags is a wonderful thing.) However, there came a point when I realised I couldn't own more without buying additional furniture for it. The thought of moving to a larger space even crossed my mind. But wait! I have a bathroom, bedroom, living room and kitchen area. I even have a spare room that I use as an office. What need did I have at this stage of my life for more? And all so I could find space to collect more statement heels? The absurdity stopped me in my tracks. But because I had these thoughts, I empathise if you have them too.

Once you discover that you're at capacity and even a wardrobe audit can't save you from the inevitable, you need to stop. Do away with those wishlists that ping you when that item is back in stock. Operate on a three out, one in policy because, let's be honest, if you can no longer house more clothing you're not in actual need of anything else.

The hoarding of clothes existed long before social media and is likely to outlive any app. However, it's undeniable that digital culture has fuelled over-con-sumption, particularly when it comes to clothing. By the very pace of which content is produced, we're groomed to subconsciously believe that constant newness is normal. Perhaps some even believe that it's a right. The problem is that these posts full of inspirational style, neatly housed within the confines of our screens, provide no context to how and where these clothes are kept.

The truth is, fashion influencers receive a copious amount of clothing. It's another flaw of an entrenched fashion industry, where brands and public relations agencies send mailers to tastemakers, hoping to get their clients featured. No fittings, sometimes no option to say no and, more often than not, no details of what the garments are made of. A vast majority of creators and editors don't have the capacity to wear or even store at the rate in which these packages come in. It's entirely unrealistic to own as many clothes as you see on the internet. In fact, I'd go so far as to say it's highly undesirable. Excess does not equate to success or happiness: the more you have, the more you're numbed to it.

Reinvest in your wardrobe through repair

'One large Chanel classic flap bag with scuffs across the body and a chunk missing from the corner.'

'White leather sandals – patch strap where it has been nibbled on the right-hand side.'

'Black slingback pumps with leather restoration required on the toe and straps.'

These are quotes from my correspondence with a repair service. All of the items mentioned had been destroyed by my 'daughter'. My daughter is a rabbit.

The pet-related destruction is a case of negligence

on my part. And you've got to admit, it's pretty niche. Luxury products are often considered specialist and can be costly to mend, just as they were expensive to purchase. However, investing in repairs is often cheaper than buying replacements. It's also the most sustainable thing you can do.

Now is a good time to address the common misconception that quality always equates to durability. This understanding is rooted in the falsehoods that fast fashion teaches us. We're so used to low price tags leading to planned obsolescence that we start to associate an investment price with an investment piece that's guaranteed to last a long time. It's not as simple as that. The fact is, the more delicate and costly an item, the higher the likelihood is that it's high maintenance too.

Most luxury experts will be honest about the limitations of goods. When I was shopping in Paris, a sales assistant at a luxury boutique politely dissuaded me from purchasing a white leather flap bag, citing its incredibly fragile nature as a deterrent. When I was reviewing new season bags, a personal shopper told me to stay away from a particular 'it' style making the rounds on social media because of how easy it is to scratch. When I discovered a particular signature bag had a new black matte hardware, an accessories buyer recommended against it as it's harder to restore and wears away quickly.

Upkeep is our duty, regardless of how much that item costs. We resent having to pay to keep a designer piece pristine but we also turn our noses up at spending £30 to restore a fast fashion item when this is almost the same price as what it costs to buy new. One of the most integral parts to saving money long term and being more sustainable is to accept full responsibility for our belongings.

So I set a challenge to any of us who have more than one item that needs alteration or repair: fix everything we already have before buying anything new. Why not reinvest in our own wardrobes? These could be items that we've loved to wear enough that there's now a tear on the inseam. We've already spent the money on those trousers with hems that pool around our shoes, so why not bring them up an inch or two and get the most use out of them? Many of us struggle to find clothes that are in our price range and cute, but the good news is we already have things to work with.

Summary

✦ How old do you feel when you're stressed about money? Instead of berating yourself, address that younger person with compassion.

✦ If you're unhappy with your spending in any area, investigate what drives it.

✦ Swap your guilty pleasures for more rewarding ones. This could involve making plans with other people to hold yourself accountable. Build a collection of experiences over objects.

✦ Try paying yourself instead of using the money for impulse buys.

✦ Use the calendar to mark off days when you didn't make any unnecessary purchases and track how much you've saved too!

Chapter 3

FASHION GOALS

I f you lost your entire wardrobe, what would be the first things you'd buy?

Personally, it would probably be underwear, a pair of socks and shoes. I want to say they'd be cute boots but realistically, I'd likely go for a pair of trainers. I'd buy a jumper or t-shirt depending on the season and trousers that could be dressed up. Jeans or a classic suit trouser would do. I'd consider how versatile those items would be so that they could be a foundation for everything succeeding them. It's likely that you'd buy something from the same categories too, perhaps in different silhouettes or colours to me as an expression of your personal taste. I suppose you could call these your wardrobe essentials. But learning what these items are isn't enough in determining your fashion goals.

Honestly, we don't even need to be in a crisis situation where we have to rebuild everything from scratch to consider the staples. We could think about what you'd pack for an overnight stay or in the event that the airline lost your suitcase what items you would need. Framing it in an extreme scenario seems to give people a clearer mind and has a strange effect of forcing them to make necessary changes.

So let's imagine we're starting from zilch. What is your manifesto as you embark on dressing yourself from scratch? Fashion goals represent your ultimate mission when you're shopping. In the context of the Mindful Monday Method, it refers to your journey in learning to make better choices for your mental health and the environment.

It also helps you cut through the noise. Have you ever been conflicted when you hear people advocate for vegan leather while others call out its high plastic content and dubious manufacturing processes? Or do you really enjoy supporting small designers but have been confused about whether it was the best option when you could opt for secondhand? There are countless other examples of points of view that don't always harmonise with one another and many people feel overwhelmed when it comes to what 'conscious consumption' looks like.

This is because almost every opinion leader in the sustainability, fashion and sustainable fashion space has their own agenda. My only motive is to help you stop impulse shopping through learning how to spot quality garments. If you want to be cynical, we can call it redemption for my influencer days. I see it as my calling for this season of my life. Now, I can't say this enough but I really have no stake in what your style preference is or how much or how little you want to spend. All journeys are valid and no one is better than any other, but it's essential that you have an idea of where you are.

My personal fashion goal is to not shop synthetics

where it's unnecessary, for the sake of circularity. By this, I don't just mean whether an item is made from a recycled material or not. I'm far more concerned with whether it can be recycled again, if it holds its value on the resale (at a charity shop or on a secondhand platform), if it can be rented out, if it can be upcycled and altered to fit your changing needs and if all else fails, whether it'll leave a low impact as it degrades. When I want to shop, I prefer to prioritise brands that are the highest quality that I can afford, especially ones that are upfront about their sustainability claims. Even if they aren't considered a 'sustainable brand' I want it to be a sustainable buy. (There's more on what this means in Chapter Five, when we discuss quality.) My goal is that I want to be so familiar with the clothes in my wardrobe that at first sight, I can tell you exactly what everything is made of.

Kind of like how you might ask me, what's your friend Caroline like? And I'll tell you how we met, our favourite spots and all of her favourite things. We should choose our clothes like we choose our friends, not only should they be as beautiful on the inside as the outside but we should know that about them. Additionally, having less clothing helps me to remember what I actually own, wear and it helps me get the most value out of it.

So what does this look like in reality? It might be different for you but essentially, I wear the same things almost every day. I have done the capsule wardrobe exercise multiple times and I see the same pieces crop up, no matter the season. It turned out that I did find my personal style through using the Mindful Monday Method, even though it's not what I created this for. I know how to shop and I know how to dress myself, but I wouldn't ever consider myself a strong stylist. The majority of us don't need to be the next Law Roach. We just want to look good and feel empowered in the clothes we wear, and I really believe that we can get you there!

What's your fashion goal?

Whether you're looking for a comfortable foothold to begin learning how to shop or you'd like some affirmation for your goals, let's start from the beginning by discovering what kind of shopper you are.

Tick which response most appeals to you. If none of them are relatable, don't check them off. At the end, add up which letter you scored the highest on. I'm going quite in depth for each of the results as I think your goals deserve a lot of attention if you're going to be set on the right path. I encourage you to read the suggestions and descriptions of the others too as, much of the time, we may have overlapping motives or want to encourage others around us to shop better.

WHAT'S YOUR FASHION GOAL?

QUIZ

You're going shopping! Where do you head to first?

A. Check out what's new from my usual go-tos
B. Start the secondhand hunt online or IRL
C. To browse designer clothes
D. I'd prefer to buy new fabric or DIY something instead

Which of these quotes best fits your values?

A. 'Make fashion work for you'
B. 'Secondhand September'
C. 'Buy less, buy better'
D. 'Loved clothes last'

How true is the statement: 'I am comfortable with being seen in the same outfit multiple times'

A. It depends who I'm with
B. That's fine, my outfits tell a story
C. Not entire outfits but specific pieces are fine
D. 100 per cent true

Which aspect of the garment production interests you the most?

A. How it's marketed or presented to customers
B. What the piece is inspired by
C. How it was put together and what it's made of
D. The environmental and social impact

A sign of a good garment is . . .

- A. One I've shopped as mindfully as possible
- B. One that inspires and defines my style
- C. One that I feel confident will last
- D. All garments are our responsibility to make 'good'!

How do you feel about trends?

- A. If it fits my style, why not?
- B. I would try to get the original, e.g. vintage
- C. As long as it's great quality
- D. I don't keep track of trends or buy them

Before you make a purchase you . . .

- A. Go on with my gut – if it doesn't suit me, I can return it
- B. Have thought of lots of ways to style it
- C. Check over the garment and compare it to other options
- D. Check that I genuinely need it

You view the wardrobe exercise as . . .

- A. A way to make getting dressed better
- B. An insight into how my personal style has developed
- C. A test of which items lasted the longest and I love the most
- D. A reminder of what I need to repair

Mostly As

Still figuring it out

The Mindful Monday Method is geared towards helping shoppers like you. You may not have a particular sustainability agenda in mind and that's OK. To want to have a better shopping experience and feel more confident in your choices is a fabulous place to start, whether that's focused around adhering to your personal tastes or aligning your buying to your understanding of ethical consumption. One of the most rewarding discoveries for those with this mindset is exploring alternative forms of shopping. Think of the magical world of preloved. Or the fantastic flexibility of rental – a great way to uncover what you really like and try on particular brands without committing to anything long term. These two alternative forms of shopping are great entry-level ways to engage with sustainable fashion because they act as a bridge for individuals who recognise discomfort with the current way that they shop and want to start with that.

I received an astute comment from someone in the Mindful Monday community. She was sharing with me how owning your visual identity goes hand in hand with learning to shop mindfully, which to her means 'looking for quality and longevity while reducing consumption where possible'. I love the way she puts it.

Maybe you have aspirations of never buying anything ever again or only wearing things from crocheters on Depop. But we need to remember that at the heart of any goal should lie the ultimate feeling of peacefulness. This can be the quiet of empowerment, knowing that your wallet isn't at the mercy of a fashion brand. The calm of confidence that you will always find a better alternative. Having this as the central focus of changing your shopping habits is essential.

Mostly Bs
Shop small, shop secondhand

Perhaps your heart sank a little when you came across the part in Chapter Two where I declared that we are not what we wear. That's not to say that you're necessarily inseparable from your visual identity – how you dress and the specific pieces you've chosen tell a story. Sometimes it's a funny memory, a talking point about a designer or something from childhood that you can't part with. Wearing it is like holding a safety blanket. You have a romance with your clothes and that's honourable, particularly when it means that you'll hold onto an item and treasure it.

The biggest celebrator of clothes is a friend and the co-founder of Fashion Revolution, Orsola de Castro, who calls shopping 'an act of pleasure'. Before I met her, I had a rather detached view of those things that we cover our bodies with. Maybe it had something to do with how emotionally affected I was by the industry that led to me pivoting careers and creating this method to cope with the shopping experience. But exploring her wardrobe – full of rips and tears, beading around moth holes and mismatched buttons to replace original ones that had fallen off – somewhat healed my cynicism.

Watching her interact with her closet was like seeing Orsola greet old friends. She introduced me to her Chopova Lowena kilt, which she was wearing way before TikTok made it cool. I made acquaintance with a reworked denim wrist bag. That was one of the first examples of upcycling that I'd seen of this high quality and it began to change my expectations of what that method is and what it could be. Seeing so many one-of-a-kind creations imbued with so much value through wear reignited a love for fashion that I hadn't realised had been washed out over the years. When I asked Orsola about her shopping preferences, she responded: 'My rule in life is if there's a charity store or thrift store – get in there. Whether it's raining or not. Because it's often that call – and then you find something incredibly perfect! So that's something I always do.'

Mostly Cs
Buy less, buy better
My only grouch (and come on, you knew I'd have one!) is the proliferation of the slogan 'buy less, buy better' when we don't really know how.

These are my simple three steps that anyone can do when trying to buy less but better:

1. Turn the garment inside out. We choose clothes like we do our friends, so it should look as beautiful on the inside as it does on the exterior.

2. Check the composition label. The Mindful Monday Method loves natural fibres because of circularity and comfort for the wearer. However, with this as your main shopping goal, you may not be as bothered with wearing synthetics as long as the piece is high quality. But for those who also have sustainability goals alongside this buy less, buy better mindset, I would still suggest avoiding synthetic blends. When it comes to mass produced fashion, a lot of the time this is used to reduce cost to manufacture – contrary to the idea they'd rather that you have, which is that plastics are primarily used to make an item more durable.

3. Refer to the wardrobe audit exercise in Chapter One. Did you recently get rid of an item just like this? Are you buying more of the same?

Using the decision trees on pages 65–7 from Chapter One is also an easy way to get to grips with how to identify a quality garment. However, as you build confidence in shopping according to your goals, you'll be able to tailor aspects of the method to best serve your needs.

Mostly Ds

Zero waste shoppers

Buying secondhand or vintage clothing items over new ones wherever possible is an ideal for many but a skill you seem to have mastered. You may not shun fast fashion brands if you happen to spot a great piece in your favourite charity shop, but they're definitely not your go-to. Sustainable fashion doesn't seem to be a challenge for you as you find the pursuit of learning how to sew and repair and discovering new techniques engages you. Handmade elements and the storytelling of clothes is an essential part of your personal style. So for those among us who love the idea of their fashion habits being as zero waste as possible, I'd like to encourage you that this could be a living reality. Here, zero waste is used as a term to describe shopping habits that try to limit disposability as much as possible – meaning making, upcycling, repairing and alterating are the most important aspects of this mindset. Shopping second-hand is important too and might be the first port of call for those who need to buy something 'new'.

Sophie Benson is a columnist for *Dazed*, an author and fashion activist who in 2022, declared that she wouldn't be buying anything at all. She had become one of the figureheads of the zero waste revolution and this is how it happened . . .

Sophie had been shopping almost exclusively from resellers on Depop and thrift stores anyway. So while her footprint might have been lower than the average consumer when it comes to fashion, it didn't address what was going on internally. You know, that spirally feeling of drowning in vertical scrolls and clothes that start to look the same. Cue the full, cold-turkey ban on shopping. The high-profile endeavour that was detailed in *British Vogue* shouldn't seem like a radical statement because as she puts it, 'It's literally doing nothing. It is the least you could possibly do.' But when the norm is not to question buying itself but what to buy, abstaining is political.

What I find most significant about a decision not to buy is the consequences of it. Frankly speaking, the only valuable calculation I can see here is looking at how much money you've saved. The real benefit is the peace that you gain as you release yourself from excess consumerism. Anyone who's ever broken up with someone who was making you unhappy knows that when you walk away from a toxic influence, what follows after is space for new connections and genuine growth. Fashion is the same.

In Benson's case, her decision to reject consumerism ended up helping her to define her style. To fulfil any wardrobe needs she had, she began turning to her dressmaking skills. 'When I was making clothes, that was what helped me understand, do I really like this silhouette, this colour or this cut? There's no way I was going to spend ten hours making something if I wasn't going to love it. So much of my fabric is secondhand and I get one shot with it, so I'm not going to waste it. That was probably more shaping in terms of personal style as opposed to abstaining from shopping.'

Beyond that valuable insight, boycotting shopping created space for community. Benson began teaching people how to crochet and sew with a machine at her local community centre. To me, this is not just revolutionary: it's actually anti-fashion.

I'll explain. The inner workings of the fashion industry are supposed to be about collaboration. It's a space where so many people work for free or very little money. We do it for the sheer love of creating beauty, magic and art. But also for the perceived glamour in the grit, hoping that enough interning or steaming in the fashion cupboards will one day land you a desk and front-row invitations to shows. The top jobs are aspirational and limited in number. So what is based on working together for the sake of art turns into something extremely hierarchical. In the case of a photoshoot, it's the photographer or stylist who is the top dog. Sometimes, the model isn't even paid. At a magazine, I'd argue it's the advertisers and the managing director who keep the entire thing from financially derailing – but if we aren't being cynical then it's the editor-in-chief who's the tastemaker and who sets the editorial tone. It's anti-fashion to educate for free. It's anti-fashion to prioritise social engagement over profit.

If you feel inspired by this and are asking yourself, 'How can I start sewing?' Sophie advises that the worst thing you can do is focus on the technical side of things and get lost in perfection. Instead, she suggests starting with something you think is really fun. 'Who cares if it's not perfect? I'm not a couturier. I just want to make things that I enjoy and I want to make sewing seem accessible for people. You can just make it up and try it to pick things apart. That is the best way to learn, instead of feeling like you have to have some formal education and know what every cut and seam is called.'

Learning how to look at quality really helps zero waste shoppers to achieve their goal of making their clothes last as long as possible. Understanding how things should be made can help many hone their upcycling prowess or get the most out of their thrifting.

Fashion goals applied IRL

In 2009, Samata Pattinson lost all of her belongings in a fire. 'I was trying to identify the damaged stuff and I honestly can't tell you what it was. It didn't mean anything. So when I started to rebuild, I was like, let me think about this differently. I didn't want to have stuff in my wardrobe that just didn't have any purpose.' Samata advocates shopping for needs 80 per cent of the time and 20 per cent for wants. 'It's not a punishment, you can still find gorgeous stuff that you love. But it's just how you're approaching it.'

Samata is also the CEO of Red Carpet Green Dress, an organisation founded by Suzy Amis Cameron that works to bring sustainability to the fashion industry through showcasing responsible fashion alternatives on the red carpet. When I asked her if her role at the sustainability-focused organisation was how she came by her fashion goals, Samata said that it did have an influence. However, it really was that life-altering trauma that shaped her mindset.

We don't often get to see successful real-life examples of what it looks like when your fashion goals align with your actions but the work that RCGD does stands out to me for that reason. The campaigns are centred around four pillars.

The first is collaborating with mainstream platforms to foster conversations and action, as Samata says, 'Otherwise we're having a siloed conversation with people who already know the subject. Mainstream is important for us because we want to reach as many people as possible.' An example of this is dressing celebrities for the Oscars and partnering with chemical company Lenzing, who produces a transparent, lower-impact viscose named TENCEL (also known as lyocell).

The second aim is to develop accessible sustainable design solutions, whereby the non-profit holds design competitions and only produces the winning look.

The third goal is to create a way of making where fashion is equitable and representative – an essential and often overlooked aspect. Feeding into that is the importance of language.

And their fourth vision: finding a way to communicate sustainability in order to facilitate change.

All of this could look like a honey-hued gown, embroidered with vintage glass beads dating from the 1920s and 30s, and dyed using goldenrod and chamomile. The design was worn by Naomie Harris in 2013 for the eighty-fifth Academy Awards. The actress had just been in *Skyfall*, a James Bond film. The dress took 120 hours to make, time logged by Dame Vivienne Westwood's couturiers, who supported the RCGD's winner, Michael Badger. Samata exclaims, 'I've never in my life seen establishing and emerging designers sharing credits on an Oscars gown. I thought that was epic.'

Another key moment for the organisation was dressing musician Billie Eilish for the ninety-fourth Academy Awards. The singer wore a custom Alessandro Michele Gucci gown created out of deadstock fabric and a repurposed nineteenth-century Fred Leighton tiara, featuring old mine- and rose-cut diamonds that could be restyled as different pieces of jewellery. Her mother, Maggie Baird, wore a dress from Benedetti Life, created with TENCEL fabric. It was pivotal because, 'You've got mother-daughter intergenerational conversation about climate and decarbonising. She's a mother of a superstar but she's a mother that's concerned about what planet she's leaving for her kid.' Fashion goals, whether they're rooted in a desire to leave minimal environmental impact or not, are always intentional. They are mindful.

Another hopeful case study that we can look to as proof that huge brands can adapt to sustainability demands is the UK retailer John Lewis Partnership.

While it's not considered a fashion company, a significant proportion of its business is based on textiles – including furniture, homeware and baby clothing. Jemima Jewell is the Head of Agriculture and Responsible Sourcing and her team is focused on circularity projects, which in this case, means shortening supply chains. One of the biggest challenges in transforming into a 'sustainable' business is untangling the supply chain, which is often opaque, outsourced and globalised. For John Lewis, a company that has traditionally invested in British business first, the ultimate goal is possibly even closing the loop – which means having a full circle from raw material sourcing (farmers), to creating the product (mill and factory), all the way to eventually repurposing that resource or perhaps even using by-product from its manufacturing for something else (recycling and upcycling). For example, the retailer uses sheep wool sourced from farmers who supply the grocery arm of the company, Waitrose & Partners, for its mattresses. The efforts promote local businesses, reduce potential waste (as British wool is not as desirable for clothing) and it means that the fibre is completely traceable.

It's about taking all 'opportunities we have to shorten and potentially close raw material loops if we reconsider our relationship with it'. In the sustainable fashion space, we often hear the saying 'it's about the journey, not the end goal' in response to the misconception that everything needs to be done perfectly. With this mission, it's about those critical first steps and here, John Lewis has started with the product categories with the highest sales volumes and highest environmental footprints. They are in the unique position of being a general goods manufacturer with a huge network based in the UK. Many brands, fashion or not, struggle without this. However, this still reveals something that others can learn from. Knowing your suppliers, keeping it 'local' and collaboration – connecting suppliers to one another – is essential to being able to make changes.

Examples of real progress exist. Red Carpet Green Dress and John Lewis are vastly different but leading the way in their own space. It's easy to be overwhelmed with the doom and gloom we hear but through numerous interviews, store visits, factory tours and speaking to brand owners, buyers, students and designers, it's clear to me that there are many people in the industry that crave genuine change.

How to think critically about fashion

The reason that defining our fashion goals is so essential is because when it comes to the vast number of methods, programmes, styling tips and even sustainability recommendations out there, things can get overwhelming and sometimes contradictory. It's important to remember that everyone has their own agenda. It's about you, the shopper, being able to take away what *you* need from whomever you choose to listen to. Here are some things to consider whenever you're faced with a claim from a brand that they're sustainable. Or even when deciding whether you should take on board the advice of an opinion leader:

- ✦ **What is the background of the person with this opinion?** For example, are they a scientist, an influencer, an activist, an editor or a brand spokesperson?
- ✦ **What is the agenda? For example, if there are any commercial motivations, do they contradict what the message is?** For example, a fashion editor is more likely to recommend clothes from brands that claim to be sustainable without looking in depth than someone in the sustainability niche with a reputation in this area. Similarly, a brand is more likely to overemphasise the benefits of what they're currently adopting, for example, its use of deadstock fabrics over many other aspects of building an ethical brand.
- ✦ **Does the means or the message sound too simplistic?** Does it leave questions unanswered? Is the language used flowery or vague?
- ✦ **Conversely, is the information presented in a complicated or overly intellectual way?** This circumstance is less common, but some brands publish enormous reports that project transparency to say a lot but in reality, saying very little. In which case, there may be other sources out there that could be more helpful.
- ✦ **Is this organisation or individual crediting other**

authority figures in the space? Do those bodies in turn endorse this entity?

✶ **Are the studies that they are referencing easily traceable?** Are they outdated (more than ten years old) and therefore need to be taken with a pinch of salt?

✶ **Are there ethical motivations that are valid but may not align with your goals?** For example, vegans will likely always opt for leather alternatives. But if it's not your lifestyle, going for secondhand, genuine leather could be a better choice.

For too long, we've sacrificed our consciousness for convenience. When it comes to learning how to shop, we cannot continue on the same path if we want to prioritise our mental and financial wellness. One of the pitfalls of maintaining the status quo is that we rely too heavily on brands or mainstream media to tell us how to spend our money. There are countless examples out there of ways to shop more sustainably (which is ironic) but none of them really address the root of the issue: that we don't have the foundational skills to do so.

I didn't always think so critically. My therapists and friends would say I am far too trusting in pretty much every aspect of my life. And of course I have fallen for misinformation, shadowy statistics or bad recommendations. Less so now, thank goodness. The great news is that most mistakes are not that deep. Most mistakes aren't permanent. My outlook in life is paralleled in how I see the fashion space – incredibly opaque. I always imagine it as navigating a maze in the dark. But acquiring knowledge about the industry and how clothes are made, understanding your wardrobe needs, your budget and your shopping goals is like having resources. They're akin to putting on the right shoes and arming yourself with a torch and a walkie talkie so that you can navigate your way through more easily. You're still in the same maze as everyone else; you've just got a lot more help and, hopefully, confidence.

When it comes to one of the most common pitfalls to dodge in this labyrinth of how to shop better, one of my pet peeves is The Formula. For example, we should only purchase X number of garments a year in order to reduce our carbon footprint. Or that the perfect wardrobe consists of 20 pieces of clothing and no more. This is something we've addressed and hopefully debunked with the Capsule Wardrobe Myth exercise in the first chapter. Then there's the theory that we should only buy something if we intend to wear it at least 30 times. I know that this approach has been helpful to many shoppers, even some of my fashion peers, as it provides room for pause in the shopping experience and has helped people to avoid unnecessary impulse buys.

But I still say, beware of using things like this as the absolute gospel to shop by. Whatever your intentions, many fast fashion pieces don't last that long, even if you don't wash them after every wear. Third-party bodies like Intertek evaluate fabric performance and give numerical ratings for light degradation, colour transfer and friction. Telling consumers to stick to somewhat arbitrary guidelines as to the number of items they can buy or own takes important focus off of the brands who are producing millions of units. Even the worst binge-buying offenders among us cannot compare to that. So the onus cannot always be placed on customers.

Another argument to do away with formulas is in-spired by journalist Megan Doyle, who writes for the likes of Fashionista, *Harper's Bazaar* UK and EcoCult. Doyle revisited the origins of '30 wears' and wrote about how it has come to be viewed as outdated. Initially, the rule of thumb was coined by pioneers Lucy Siegle, a journalist and BBC reporter, and Livia Firth, a co-founder and creative director of Eco-Age. This was in 2015, when the fashion industry was barely flirting with the idea of transparency and environmentalism, let alone making any firm commitments. When it was first popularised, it was necessary to provide a framework to work with and build on. Since then, much has changed.

The Covid-19 pandemic has been a huge accelerator for changes in consumption. It challenged individuals to consider what was truly important when faced with financial and emotional uncertainty. This was noticeable even in my corner of social media. From 2019 until the middle of 2021, when I talked about how things are made and its impact on us and the planet, it was a niche conversation. But as the UK emerged from mandated lockdowns, it was noticeable how much people wanted to take action and shop less, for good. Now the hashtag #mindfulmondaymethod has over 24.3 million views at the time of writing. More significant than my own experience of change, Google reported that in 2022, US searches for 'how to reduce waste' and 'waste less' peaked at a record number (although what that was wasn't disclosed).[xiv]

The reason formulaic approaches are no longer effective is because we've graduated from this. There is multi-generational motivation to save money and be more conscious about our environmental impact. We are looking for more meaningful, longer-term solutions and, if possible, ones that allow us to be more creative.

It's not just because I think formulas are restrictive and passé that I don't want to promote them. It's often because it's followed by the intent to sell you something you don't need. It was late morning in February when my friend sent me an article. I could see from the thumbnail that it was a written piece espousing an ideal figure for the number of new clothes that one should purchase per year in order to reduce their carbon footprint. I didn't want to click it out of principle (as you have gathered, I can't stand this sort of thing) but I felt that perhaps I may learn something . . . The short story is: I didn't. When I got to the bottom of the slick and beautifully designed article, I noticed that most of the advice was followed up with a shopping edit of what that individual *should* buy.

Commercial motivations aren't a bad thing. It is what the entire publishing industry is funded by and audiences do want help with their purchases. But here's some advice for the future, if you are to come across a formulaic method like this again, as I'm sure you will: anything that encourages you to rely on the opinion of others more than it aids you to use your own critical thinking is not worth listening to. Only you know what you need the most. We may move countries, get married (do your wedding outfits count as one of the allotted garments for the year?) or discover that another style expresses us better. Worse still, with a formula-based method, we aren't practising any discernment like checking labels or examining seams and finishes.

Can we trust sustainability tools?

A consumer-facing example of a useful sustainability tool is the app and website Good On You. It stands out particularly as it has managed to dodge the bullet of becoming a tool for greenwashing. It's an educational platform that looks at what should constitute an ethical fashion company, using over 500 data points to judge impact on three categories: people, planet and animals. The brands are then rated from 'we avoid' to 'great'. Good On You also suggests alternative places to shop based on companies that have scored higher. I would recommend taking a look at this if you're at the start of your sustainable shopping journey, particularly to get comfortable with the basics of what 'conscious' brands should cover. However, make up your own mind about where these brands sit on your scale. What I like about Good On You is that it's not something that brands can easily utilise and distort to their advantage. Mostly because the scores of these retail giants can't compete with universally recognised sustainable brands like People Tree or Nudie Jeans.

People Tree is one of the long-standing sustainable brands that was doing its part even before it was cool. It's a member of the World Fair Trade Organization, which requires independent auditing and regular reviews. It's also PETA approved and boasts not one but two organic badges at the time of writing (Global Organic Textile Standard and Soil Association). If there's an accreditation, this brand will go after it.

Now, bearing badges of honour from third parties is not the only thing that makes a sustainable brand. Huge companies can slap a couple of organic certifications on their websites too – you might've seen the likes of Global Organic Textile Standard (GOTS) or Better Cotton Initiative (BCI). These are often extremely costly and smaller businesses can't afford the bragging rights, so don't discount all independents simply because they haven't bought the luxury. In many ways, this is considered a 'pay to play' by sustainability experts. But on the flipside, having recognisable certifications like being able to use Forest Stewardship Council (FSC) on a label or emblazoned on a website does make it easier to convince shoppers to feel confident in what they're purchasing.

There is one event in particular that prompted brands to reevaluate the way that they use sustainability tools to communicate their progress, and simultaneously revealed to customers just how murky the water of greenwashing really is. I'm referring to the Higg Index, which rebranded to Worldly in 2023. Established in 2011 by the Sustainable Apparel Coalition (SAC), it's made up of 270 members which include C&A, Boohoo, Artizia and Zalando, to name a few. Higg positioned itself as 'a single source for ESG [environmental, social and governance] performance data' for apparel and footwear companies. There's a cost involved for the companies to access the tools needed to assess themselves.

They are based on a scale from 0 to 100, with higher scores indicating better sustainability performance. However, just a decade on, and after behemoths like Tommy Hilfiger, H&M and Levi's adopted it (mostly its own members), holes started appearing as critics dug into it, noting how the index didn't do enough to hold brands accountable for their supply chain issues. Mostly, Higg became a facade behind which businesses could operate as usual. There were many criticisms, as might be expected of a giant undertaking like this attempting to cover so much ground and so early on with very little regulation, and the system was largely discredited.

Closely following this industry-wide blow up came whispers of a new approach to communicating sustainability goals . . . which looks like not communicating sustainability goals. This is called greenhushing, when companies don't talk about their environmental practices because they're afraid of the backlash. This comes less from a place of shyness and uncertainty, and is instead more about businesses realising that they're not doing enough so they try not to attract any attention to themselves. Kind of like when I used to shrink to the back of the gym when people picked their sports teams because I knew I couldn't (and wouldn't) pull my weight. Except in my case, it really was for the sake of my poor teammates and my dignity. In the case of greenhushing, it's about shirking corporate responsibility.

Then there's the B Corp certification, short for 'Benefit Corporation', another voluntary certification that involves a rigorous self-assessment and audit across five categories. These are governance, workers, customers, community and the environment. The scoring system requires a minimum of 80 out of 200 points for a company to be certified. Like the other certifications, there's a fee attached to becoming a B Corp, which is charged on a sliding scale according to revenue. Some companies have told me that they've needed to assign an entire role just to pass the evaluation as it's so thorough. It's worth noting that while B Corp can do wonders for the reputation of a brand, it doesn't guarantee that all of its products are 'sustainable' to everyone, because as we've learnt by now, this doesn't really exist. I've reviewed clothes from a number of retailers that have this status but many of its products don't align with the fashion goals of zero waste, shopping small and circularity perspectives. However, it's still a brilliant sign and encouraging that, as of 2021, globally there are over 4,000 certified B Corps in 150 industries and 70 countries.

It's important to remember that sustainable fashion remains highly unregulated and while legislations are in the works to create some form of standardisation, everyone's just trying to work out the best course of action in whichever area they're in. Many companies are retrospectively having to amend their ways so it's not entirely fair to write off mammoth efforts like Worldly or B Corp. Yes, brands use them somewhat as marketing tools but it's also a step towards bringing transparency to a notoriously opaque industry. So, can we trust them? I believe that they're useful in the context of the Mindful Monday Method but not the be all and end all of our decision making process.

Rental fashion

Rental businesses have been around since the early 2000s. The US fashion 'members club' Rent the Runway started in 2009. About a decade later, several UK counterparts popped up all around the same time. Adoption has been hyper fast and Victoria Prew, the CEO of HURR, the world's first rental fashion company to achieve B Corp status, says, 'Circular models in their entirety are expected to account for up to a third of customers' closets in the next ten years.' What I find so intriguing about the rental model is how closely it resembles the relationship between publicity houses and publications and VIPs when it comes to loaning clothing.

I recall one of the first times I saw rental clothes in real life. It was around the time of the pandemic when the concept was quite novel. I attended a press day, which is when public relation companies or brands will showcase what they have available that season. I hadn't ever seen the glitzy occasionwear pieces beyond the confines of an iPhone screen before and wondered what they looked like in real life. I actually expected the experience to be something similar to a PR showroom. Visiting one of these is always interesting, at least for me. Usually, you're greeted by the PR associate who invited you. Everyone else in the office is either typing away at their keyboards, steaming garments or tackling the ever-present pile of boxes at the back of the room. When you see the clothes, there's an aura of cool, almost like you're in a museum of clothes rather than a shop or what it is – a showroom. There's a distance between you and the garments. You don't know each other yet. As you browse and your mind begins to fill in the possibilities and opportunities of wearing these creations, you run your fingers across all the textures – crinkled silk, embroidered tulle, lace, sequin, feather and leather . . . then something special catches your eye. There's a hit of dopamine; your heartbeat jumps a little.

So yeah, my first encounter with rental fashion was

nothing like that. Actually, I was slightly horrified at what I saw. Sparkly, wonderful things hung side by side. From afar, it looked exactly like it did in photos! Up close, though, I realised I was looking at fraying, glittering dresses, figure-hugging knits with seams splitting, designer dresses reeking of chemicals and tiny tears. I felt catfished. It was heartbreaking to see what were once beautiful clothes left in such disrepair. I pointed out that there was quite a bit of damage to some of the pieces and the girl showing me around simply shrugged. It wasn't her fault but I felt a little jaded – surely a circular business might want to go about mending the things under its care?

I'm not here to simply sing the praises of every cool development in the name of sustainable fashion. I'll always first and foremost think about how it benefits you, the shopper.

The truth is, quite a lot of clothes aren't suited to the gruelling process of constant wearing. I'm all for getting that cost per wear in, but within context. Clothes need to be honoured for what they are and many occasion-wear pieces are delicate. Luckily, this was just one experience. Seeing other companies display their wares in public has given me confidence that that incident was likely an anomaly.

Renting an outfit can be a universally great option, no matter which fashion goal you identify with the most. If you're wondering how it works, as an example, let's take a wedding invitation. Often, those lucky individuals who get multiple save the dates through their letterbox are considering that they'll bump into the same people from their social circles. It's important to remember that everyone's too busy thinking about themselves to notice incidents of outfit repeating. But I can empathise with the anxiety. I've never doubted my wardrobe since practising my own methodology. However, I have to admit that there was a recent time where the constant chatter of a friend's strict dress code for her wedding became the topic of conversation for an entire bachelorette trip. I started strong – for the first 48 hours, I resisted the notion that I was lacking anything to wear. After three days, I started to question if I even owned any clothes. Peer pressure is real and nothing is more inflammatory than a social event with the guarantee of photography.

When it comes to rental, a customer can search on any of the platforms available in their country or city. UK-based HURR has its own rental website but the company also currently powers the rental capabilities of luxury retailer Matches Fashion and high-end department store Selfridges, amongst others. You might look there if you're feeling fancy and wanting the reassurance of a professionally managed inventory, where the rental platform is responsible for cleaning and sending the customer clothes on schedule. The other option might be to rely on another person to be responsive to your request to rent pieces from their wardrobe.

You can filter your search according to designer, size,

availability and take a look at the items of clothing that interest you. Often, both renters and the owners of the clothes will have a rating. Depending on where you rent from, users may also have the option of speaking to the person who's interested in wearing their cocktail dress. It breeds a sense of community and trust – when I rented a pink feather Cult Gaia dress for a trip to Barcelona, I more than welcomed its owner telling me to be aware of the plumes getting caught in the zip! Once you mutually agree to the fee, length of time and provide delivery and return addresses, the renter simply waits for their parcel to arrive at the door. Once time is up with the garments, they're returned.

The business of rental

Rental fashion companies usually follow these models: peer-to-peer, past season inventory from brands, buying inventory, subscription-based services or partnering with a retailer or brand to rent current season stock. The combination of the above strategies does influence how circular they can really be. After all, it's this element of keeping clothing in use as long as possible and responsibly managing them that makes the basis of their sustainability claims.

There are some rental models that involve individuals or the companies themselves to purchase clothes to rent to customers and these face the issue of having to constantly buy new items. Having closely followed the rise of the UK fashion rental companies, I've seen founders talk about no longer stocking a particular style from a brand because it's simply too delicate to be worn multiple times and go through rigorous cleaning. Not all clothes are suitable for rental. It could be that they're simply not good enough quality or they're well-made but far too fragile. When it comes to peer-to-peer structures, the owner of the garment will be able to discern when it is beyond repair. It's pretty hard for a rental company with owned inventory (as opposed to borrowing past season items from retailers or relying on peer-to-peer rentals) to pull an item from its site before making their money back. Another problem these businesses may face is needing to embrace microtrends. Whatever the latest luxury brand-meets-sportswear collaboration is or what a Kardashian was photographed in last week becomes a priority. Renting is better in this scenario, than each of us going out and buying our own without knowing when we'll wear it again. However, it works better when we can rent directly from the brand, as it would ideally encourage less production (at least that is the long-term hope). And this would address the root of the issue, rather than looking at it in a reductive way that focuses mainly on the shoppers. Not all rental models are equal. Not all of them are as 'sustainable' as they could be.

Another option is for brands to launch their own subscription service. Logistically, this system isn't desirable for every brand, not to mention that not many can afford to do this. But it makes sense that the companies large enough in size and with adequate geographical distribution to fulfil these orders are trying. When considering sustainability as a journey, these creative solutions are welcome.

However, it does raise questions about brand reputation. Will associating luxury clothing with a subscription based purchasing model dilute its status? Will this pivot to accepting the ownership of clothing as temporary and transient impact its quality? It remains to be seen whether this circular approach will impact the volume of production from brands themselves. To me, this is the ultimate measure of whether or not it's a viable solution for the sustainability agenda and only time will tell. For shoppers, I wonder if it opens the possibility for true minimalism to become mainstream. To conclude, I have a question for you. Do you like the idea that in the future, we will own just our wardrobe staples and everything else can be shared?

Is this really sustainable?

Some of the same problems that plague the retail industry carry forward to rental businesses too. These include the issue of logistics, dry cleaning and of course, size inclusivity. I'm hoping that some of these hurdles are more teething pains than long-term problems that will go ignored. Interestingly, these are also points of critique for those keen to pick at its sustainability credentials, but I believe we should be hopeful.

Picture this: you have an event coming up and you've

decided that you're going to try out fashion rental. There are several concerns that arise as you fill in your payment details and await an email confirmation. Firstly, there's the thought of whether it'll arrive in time. Secondly, will it fit? Thirdly, what if I spill wine all over this?

Unfortunately, rental businesses can't do too much to help you when accidents happen, but there are safeguards in place. After all, it's a relatively new concept and people can be nervous to mail their favourite jacket to a stranger's address. Whenever friends express this to me, I imagine them waiting by a window, forlornly counting down the days for their items to come back in one piece (and preferably not wrapped in a plastic grocery bag, which I have experienced before. The item was returned OK, though, and I found it kind of funny). Many say that they will pay up to full RRP of items if they're damaged beyond repair or proven to be stolen, although this isn't widely advertised and is more something I've found out through collaborating with a few of these businesses for my job. Whether or not they uphold it and how they fulfil it is another story.

As to the concern about sizing – well, this seems to be the biggest cited reason for normal refunds, why wouldn't it plague the rental system too? GANNI, a fashion brand that also offers rental, addressed the topic of sizing via its Instagram page @ganni.lab. The Danish brand's bio cites its goal as 'working on becoming a more responsible version of ourselves'. GANNI calculated that only 8 per cent or 61 out of a whopping 780 options in its online collection (in March 2023) could be found in extended sizing.[xv] It's an interesting example because very few brands would publicise these sorts of statistics, but information such as this can really help us to visualise the extent of challenges when driving forward the sustainable fashion agenda. However, it demonstrates a pervasive problem that is echoed in rental companies too. If brands that own their own stock don't do enough to create an inclusive size range, how can rental businesses that rely on said brands and peer-to-peer wardrobes be able to offer inclusivity in their inventory?

Another echo of a problem in the wider fashion industry that we see in rental businesses is a reluctance to represent curvy bodies in marketing and social media visuals. Fashion and lifestyle creator Charlotte Jacklin is based in the UK and before her influencer days, she worked for several of the largest British fashion brands. '[Fashion companies] are saying there's not an audience for it, but they never roll these things out correctly. They never make it really apparent on their social media, on their website or on their e-commerce' – which discourages potential customers.

In other words, retailers like to use data points as a deflection of why they don't invest more in catering to plus size bodies. During some of my store visits where I meet brand founders, I often ask them what the size run is. So often, I hear the feedback that customers simply don't ask for plus sizes. The brands say that they'll cater to the voices that they receive feedback from. But it's a chicken-and-egg situation, if it's not available and you don't make people feel welcome, why would they engage at all? I can't help but feel that this is a cop out.

When it comes to rental, friends who are plus-size have told me they have struggled to find options and feel that they have to settle for things instead of being excited to wear something. Abisola Omole, who we met in Chapter One, shares the same sentiment: 'I find that there's just not a lot of choice as it's a peer-to-peer platform. It means that stock is what other people have. And there's still just not a lot of pieces. Because there aren't that many plus sized people who are able to get a certain calibre of dress, and this leads to the accessibility side of things – and I'm not even talking about price range.'

It's not a true solution, but rental companies not charging a customer if the clothes don't work for them is one of my favourite, simplest responses to a prevalent challenge. Ultimately, the onus lies not on the customer or renter but fashion retailers to step up. If brands truly believe in circularity, then they cannot make it easier for straight-sized individuals than plus-sized ones to access their rental inventory.

The other point of contention when it comes to rental is the operations. Specifically the delivery and dry cleaning that the business model relies on. The 'last mile' is something that rental businesses struggle with as much as traditional retailers do. This refers to the last leg of a product's journey, from the warehouse to what is often the customer's doorstep. It's a complex and expensive part of retail that makes up a significant amount of the total delivery cost.

HURR has partnered with Packfleet, a delivery company that wants to set itself apart by hiring its employees full-time as opposed to on zero-hour contracts, a common employment model that has been slated for its unethical implications. It also invests in the B Corp scheme. Rental isn't inherently sustainable. But to avoid it for the same logistical issues that the rest of the fashion industry faces isn't productive either.

OK, let's talk about dry cleaning. The issue with the cleaning process is the chemical perchloroethylene, otherwise known as PERC, is an incredibly effective substance used for removing stains on clothing. The Centers for Disease Control and Protection (CDC) notes that 'the skin is a less important absorption site', meaning that it's not at risk of taking in the toxic chemicals. Instead, the CDC notes that the real threat is through inhaling PERC. It's still currently widely used in the UK, in spite of knowing the risks. However, in the state of New York, use of the chemical is highly regulated. The CDC also published the findings of a study that looked at the long-term effects of PERC on dry cleaning employees. The case study undertaken by National Institute for Occupational Safety and Health (NIOSH) spans from the 1960s to 1996. Findings show that exposure to PERC causes an alarmingly elevated risk of cancer, although it's also careful to point out that there were other chemicals involved over the course of this time.[xvi]

'Eco' dry cleaning innovations have arisen, such as Oxwash in the UK, which reportedly saves around 60 per cent of the water versus a typical commercial washing machine. Importantly, the company also uses biodegradable detergents. If you've never heard of that before, don't worry because it's incredibly niche. Essentially, this kind of cleaning solution doesn't contain 'harmful contaminants' when it breaks down, so it shouldn't pollute water or irritate our skin. There are improvements across all aspects of fashion, even in spaces as niche as cleaning, which is often an afterthought of our shopping experiences!

I polled my audience and asked them what their main motivation for renting clothes is. I gave them the choices 'to be more sustainable', 'to try new brands', 'to experiment with my style' or 'to try what it's all about'. It was a close call but the two most cited responses were to make more sustainable choices (as opposed to shopping for new clothes) and to use it as a way to experiment with their style. It overlaps with the possibility of trying out a new brand but this speaks more to visual identity, unconstricted by the prospect of a difficult returns process or budget.

Whenever something disrupts the status quo, you can bet there will always be resistance. It's part and parcel of testing the viability of something new and this can actually be beneficial to businesses. After all, if there's no challenge to the claim that something like rental fashion is a sustainable route for consumption, how can those who truly want to do better actually act on their concerns? One of the biggest critiques of the whole system is that it's not a better alternative to shopping at all because of how much water, toxic chemicals and single-use plastic are used in the dry cleaning process. Not to mention the transportation and logistics of posting clothes around the country, often with strict time restraints. However, those who celebrate the rental model often point to the stats around creating new clothes, a process which has a significantly higher environmental impact.

Overall, renting can be joyous. It can bring that spark to a dying, jaded relationship that you might have slipped into with fashion. Renting offers a monetary benefit to those who have heaving wardrobes or at least own a few buzzy, in-demand designer labels.

The lust for something new and novel won't go away any time soon. It will take time to undo the impact of the fashion industry's decades of advertising (maybe it's just capitalism). Shoppers still want to wear something fresh and renting fashion is a great weaning option. Rental fashion has a firm place in the future of fashion, but it may not always look how it does now. One of the reasons I find the rise of rental fashion fascinating even though I've never believed it to be a solution to the fast-fashion problem is that it challenges our perception of ownership. It forces us to view fashion as the binder of a wide network of humans. We are not defined by what we wear or what we possess. It also reinforces the idea that the clothes on our backs are connected to one another and can be experienced in different ways. It humanises the experience of participating in fashion, something that the industry has stripped with its FOMO advertising and unrealistic (quite literally when you consider the use of AI models) beauty standards.

Shopping preloved

When I was a teenager, I had pages torn from *Vogue* plastered across my room as wallpaper. Vintage fashion was having a resurgence of 'cool' – Kate Moss and her impeccable style is to thank for that. I have the image of her in a diaphanous slip dress seared onto my brain. Back then, even though my pocket money couldn't stretch that far, I was dying to visit Annie's, where I had once read that the supermodel shopped at. When I finally got my parents to take me, I discovered a treasure trove of lace gloves, flapper dresses and secondhand fur coats.

Fashion's craze for vintage and preloved items died out for a few years during my late teens and early twenties. There became a segregation between ultra high-end pieces that would be glorified and charity shop finds that held very little status at all. Clothing is officially considered to be vintage if it was made 20 to 100 years ago, although the term is used very loosely now for anything that looks 'of an era' and denotes a style.

Whether or not you're a fierce defender of the proper use of the word 'vintage', even when used interchangeably, secondhand and vintage still have different connotations. It's frustrating because many shoppers wouldn't be able to discern between them, so we know it's a stigma that needs to be broken down.

There are certain demographics and cultures, such as my own for example, that may not feel as comfortable with buying preloved as their first choice. The most common negative idea about secondhand shopping is that it's for those that can't afford to buy new. I posed the question 'What do your families think of secondhand fashion as a person of colour (POC)?' to my audience and almost all the responses reflected that belief.

Even within my own family, secondhand clothing held superstitious connotations, not just ideas about social status. I was reminded of that when so many respondents said that their parents believed that 'if you don't know where it's come from, there's a fear of bad energy' or that they're 'against it because they're scared of bad luck', which could also be specific to items like shoes. What also stuck out to me was the number of responses that said, 'dead people clothes', which we know is unlikely, given the rate that individuals (who are very much alive and spending) buy and discard their clothing.

The most frequent answer was 'unhygienic' and 'dirty', although exceptions were made when clothes were passed down through family members. Almost half of these individuals were quick to follow up that their parents have since changed their minds, impressed with what great-value gems they've been able to discover.

The good news is that the divide between the concepts of vintage being cool and secondhand fashion being second tier is slowly closing. The 2022 Resale Report by online thrift store Thredup projected the US resale market to reach $82 billion by 2026. So not only are perceptions on secondhand clothing altering across generations but globally too. Thanks to social media and marketplaces like Depop, the pursuit of preloved is glamorised. The UK-based shopping app started gaining momentum around 2015–16, based on Google search trends, and is particularly popular among Gen Z. In 2021, Etsy acquired the platform for around $1.6 billion USD.[xvii] Wilson Griffin of Recurate, a tech company that builds resale platforms onto e-commerce sites, said that in 2022, resale grew 11 times faster than traditional retail. Similar to how many retailers are incorporating a rental structure into their business model, we're seeing a trend of established brands incorporating an archive or resale element too.

As for charity shops, one afternoon, I moseyed into my favourite one in Kensington. I was taken in by an incredible pink shearling coat and just had to find out how much it cost. It led to me talking to a very enthusiastic sales assistant who told me about the pricing system and how donations are valued at roughly around third of the retail price. She explained that there are variables, such as whether the item is new, if the garments still have tags on or if it was incredibly expensive to begin with. In the case of the amazing designer outerwear, it retailed for over £2,800, but there was no way they could price it at £900. It was listed for £650 and the next week, when I returned to see what they had in stock, it had sold.

Aside from that piece, the prices at that charity shop range from around the £20–£60 mark, although almost all the labels bear recognisable brand names. I was told that up to 30 new items are introduced to the shop floor daily, but how much is donated and the quality of it varies greatly from day to day. Clothes are marked with the week that they were donated. If they remain unsold, they're circulated around their other retail sites and undergo gradual discounting. The price is dictated by the charity's head office, as opposed to sweet volunteers guessing how much an item is worth. (I don't disclose the names of these charity shops as these conversations took place as a customer, not an author. Similar to how I reference my in-store brand reviews when I discuss quality, take these anecdotes not as the ultimate truth but a reflection of my experience.)

I spoke to another charity shop in the area and was told that very few donated items are in a fit condition for resale. These need to be taken away by a rag and bone man. This waste is precisely what contributes to the £140 million of clothing that is sent to landfill in the UK every year. The slightly problematic and outdated notion that we're 'clothing less fortunate people' when we give away our tatty fast fashion, this needs to die a cold, hard death. And if you thought that the UK takes responsibility for its own textile waste, think again.

One of the most infamous secondhand markets is Kantamanto in Accra; it receives a reported 15 million garments a week. With volume like this, clothes are bought in bales. Resellers don't always know what they're going to get. The OR Foundation is a leading registered charity in Ghana that tackles waste colonialism in this particular region. Waste colonialism is defined as 'domination of one group of people in their homeland by another group through waste and pollution'.[xviii] In short, how the Global North doesn't want the ecological disasters associated with trash, so it exports it to become another country's environmental problem. It's not a cute look.

In a revealing video series created for social media, the organisation sent delegates from Kantamanto to the very origins of these clothes: fast fashion shops. 'The quality of the product from day one, from manufacturing, is bad,' says Solomon Noi about his experience walking through H&M. Another, Abena Essoun, a former Kantamanto retailer, comments that the clothes look like they'd last 'a couple wears before they rip apart', so by the time that they reach the market in Ghana, they aren't even wearable or resaleable. It is quite literally rubbish.

I hope you can understand now that most clothes are not worth buying at all , which is how we've ended up with overflowing charity shops, and that even when we shop preloved, it's essential to check the garment over. It's not about boycotting, I would never suggest that, especially when it comes to supporting a charity. It's also not about being ascetic, self-righteous or depriving yourself. It is really about refusing to settle for less.

Tips for shopping secondhand

Buying secondhand isn't a free pass to shopping more sustainably. We need to be mindful about what we're buying (which means checking those composition labels!) and the volume of which we're purchasing.

Take a look at these tips on how to shop preloved:

* When shopping on websites with a seller rating system, pay attention to the reviews. For eBay, a good number to go for is above 98 per cent positive reviews.
* Google Image search is your friend. If you can't find images (for example, from archive runway galleries) of the item to compare the secondhand listing to then reverse search it on the engine to

find out the original price, what it looks like in a brand new condition, what the composition is if the care label has been removed and if any reviews of what the product is like exist out there.

✳ Look for original photos, no matter how grainy or badly lit they are. If the seller uses e-commerce visuals to accompany the product listing, that's fine. But receiving a user picture is useful in gauging what kind of condition it's really in. From personal experience, I've found that listings with photos that were taken by the seller are usually in a better condition when I see the item in real life.

✳ When shopping preloved in real life, affluent neighbourhoods in the biggest cities have the best charity shop stock but the prices will usually reflect the area its in – the fancier the postcode, you may expect to see a slightly higher price tag.

✳ Thrift+ is a great marketplace selling donated items and proceeds go to a charity of their choice. If you don't have access to great secondhand options where you live, try this online destination.

Upcycling

Upcycling is the act of remaking an existing garment into something else. It is one of the notable things that has come out of the resurgence of interest in used clothing. Colloquially it is known as 'thrift flipping'. This involves finding garments from charity shops and flea markets, repairing or altering them to be more desirable and selling them for a profit. A remarkable movement that has revived sewing as a covetable skill and celebrates creativity.

The popularity of secondhand clothing is also rooted in an entrepreneurial spirit, which further democratises fashion. Now, people no longer need to have studied fashion (or have attended university at all), or be of a certain age to run an online business. I often feel I would've been a happier, less self-conscious teenager had I been born ten years later.

However, selling repurposed clothing has attracted a lot of criticism: mostly that upcyclers are driving up the prices of secondhand clothing, buying larger sizes that are already in short supply and creating a lot of potential textile waste in the process. Popular upcycling projects include halving large button downs or t-shirts to join with another colourway or pattern for a mismatched look. Then there's slicing a men's suit jacket to create a cropped half and a mini skirt. Ultimately, in determining whether or not this is a sustainable endeavour that you'd like to support, it's about looking at where and how businesses responsibly source their textile. The majority of used clothing is sold by the bale, by wholesalers or even at kilo sales so paid by weight as opposed to per item. It's not the most economical choice for any upcycling business to source directly from thrift shops.

There are clearly more than enough garments to go round – whether something is sold to us by a savvy teenager online or we dug around clearance bins at Cancer Research to find it.

Another point to consider is the quality of the upcycled product and whether a perfectly good garment has been adapted to fuel the demand for a micro trend. Upcycling for private consumption, is another story, absolutely no one would stand in your way if you wanted to experiment.

However, it's still important to consider how well a garment is constructed first and foremost and avoid the pitfall of viewing upcycling as synonymous with being sustainable. A great example of fashion designers that use this skill creatively is Ukrainian brand Ksenia Schnaider, who created 'denim fur' from frayed cotton, which resembles a shag. Or British designer Conner Ives that revitalises vintage garments and deadstock material into wonderful, contemporary creations. Another is Marine Serre, a popular French label that's known for its identifiable crescent logo. The brand has a few lines that repurposes textile like old tea towels and aprons into beautiful new clothes.

Secondhand luxury

It's been somewhat of an uphill battle for the second-hand market to climb its way into the higher echelons of fashion's consciousness, and even longer until I caught on to what a wonderful world it is. Growing up in a Chinese household had an impact on how I viewed preloved clothing. I mean, this is a culture that encourages a whole new wardrobe every lunar new year for good luck. (I don't partake in this; while I respect the tradition, I find that wearing something I already own but styling it a different way will suffice.) My family couldn't understand my fascination with the secondhand craze while I was growing up and, unfortunately, as it fell out of the trend cycle so did my interest. I watched from afar, an interested observer who didn't quite know how to participate. But my mind changed drastically when I did a 'Wardrobe Raid' on my friend Camilla.

If you're unfamiliar with that, it's where I visit someone's closet in real life and review it. The Mindful Monday Method is supposed to be adapted to an individual's needs and it's fascinating to see how it plays out in real life.

So this is how it works: my case studies choose the items that they want my opinion on. It's so important to respect people's purchase decisions, so I rely on them to pick things out. I don't go charging into their private spaces, pointing out every wonky hemline. As someone who's very small and takes up a lot of her trouser legs, I can guarantee you'll spot a dropped blind seam or badly cut raw hem if you take the time to look at mine. There are types of garments that come up quite often, such as pieces bought from cult designers that didn't live up to the hype. Or, on the other hand, special garments with beautiful details that they're proud to show me. I'm often presented with items that people know were a bad buy but they need to find out *why* they hate it so much.

But in the case of Camilla's wardrobe, every single item that flew out of those doors was pure magic. I imagine that each morning, her clothes swirl about her in swathes of ephemeral cloud and glitter, like when Cinderella transforms into her ball gown. (That dress exists in her collection, by the way. It's a shimmering blue off-the-shoulder Elie Saab number.) There was a sweetheart neck-line gingham number that looked like it was made of 100 different panels, which created the most gorgeous sculpted silhouette. And a vintage Oscar de la Renta piece with a built-in boned bodice. Oh, and my absolute favourite – her collection of Dior bar jackets in 100 per cent wool with silk lining. I saw enough clothing from that Wardrobe Raid to cover two videos and it still barely scrapes the floral chiffon surface of her museum. And the reason I describe all of this with such fervour is that almost all of it is secondhand. It was this encounter that made me fall in love with the beautiful universe that is vintage designer. A safe haven amidst the polyester lining, exposed over-locks and poorly fitted clothes I'm exposed to every week in my real life, in-store reviews.

The first thing I bought came from the French luxury marketplace, Vestiaire Collective. It was a fantastically bright neon pink jacquard coat with diamantes on the buttons. It's so incredible you'd have thought Barbie designed it in her dreams.

But it's vintage Yves Saint Laurent, actually. I scored that for just under £200. Next was a well-tailored Jean Paul Gaultier jacket in a Prince of Wales check. It cost £80 including shipping. I remember recording myself opening it and I was crossing my fingers that none of my biases would be true: that it would smell of body odour or moth balls, be peppered with snagging and the worst of all – sweat stained lining. After absolutely none of that occurred, I caught the bug.

If you're not well versed with the world of secondhand luxury, I understand that these do seem like high prices. And to be frank – because over here we are nothing but – spending money is never saving money. But when you consider that a high street blazer costs around £70–£100 and won't survive more than a season, I hope we can agree that I got a good deal. Several of them.

Vintage luxury helped me to fall in love with fashion again. It reminded me that quality still existed and at a fraction of the price. It showed me that value doesn't only come from the status of the name on the label, the time it takes to make something or the cost of the raw material used – there's also an integral element of storytelling. Not just of the history of the piece, because not everyone wants or has a garment that has a colourful backstory, but how you acquired it and what it says about your personal style. What I love about preloved clothing is that there's no validation from the masses. If you like it, you really like it. The beauty of it is that it is very unique.

Secondhand luxury fashion isn't always fun and games. There was a time that I got burnt in the form of a fake Versace skirt. Luckily, quality speaks volumes and knowing how to shop helps you discern genuine articles from counterfeit products, even if you're unfamiliar with the ins and outs of all the luxury names. It's also helpful to shop with reliable sources. Sites like Vestiaire Collective offer authenticity checks before the item reaches the buyer. eBay has an authentication guarantee for specific luxury products. Many designer resellers use Entrupy, an AI-driven verification technology that claims to be 99.1 per cent accurate to authenticate the goods. However, after I (easily, I might add) got my money back from purchasing the dud garment, I turned to my vintage expert friend, Thidarat Kaha from Archive Six, for advice on how shoppers can be more discerning.

I first met Tee while browsing her pop-up space on Oxford Street. My TikTok account was just gaining traction and I was receiving a constant stream of requests for brand recommendations, something I have and always will struggle with being able to provide. My number one reason for not being able to do this is that quality is so inconsistent, even within a single brand. Don't worry if that's confusing, we'll get into this in Chapter Five. But this isn't such a problem with vintage clothing. If an item has survived this long, it's generally pretty well made and its condition is more of the concern.

Archive Six specialises in the kind of designers the supermodels wore in the late 1990s and early 2000s. Jean Paul Gaultier, Vivienne Westwood, Moschino and Versace are names that you'll encounter when flicking through Tee's highly curated racks. I discovered that when you become an established name in this space, you tend to have your 'thing' – such as a particular era or a brand that you know a lot about. Determining whether an item with a designer label is real or not doesn't require you to go to a specialist school or acquaint yourself with a forensics kit. A lot of the time, following your common sense and not getting swept up in the hopes of a great deal can help.

I discovered that my Versace safety pin skirt was indeed a fake after noticing a wonky hemline with a thread nest and paint peeling from the hardware. There was no care label nor any sign that it had been removed. The skirt was a newish season piece, so it would've had the holographic label too. One of the key takeaways I got from speaking to Tee was that vintage luxury resellers are absolute die-hard fanatics of their chosen niche, whether that be a certain era or designer. If you're buying from a small independent rather than a large platform, more likely than not the person running the business will be more than happy to educate you on the piece you're bringing home. Follow my tips on how to look out for genuine luxury goods but also, trust your gut and feel good about who you're purchasing from. Don't be swayed by the temptation of a 'good price'. I'd also like to add, as someone with an incredibly soft spot for rescue dogs, shopping vintage or in fact, secondhand at that, reminds me of the slogan, 'Adopt Don't Shop'. There are so many gorgeous garments in existence that are still looking for homes, don't be afraid to start here first!

Tips for shopping vintage clothing

* Comparison is key. If you already have an item from a similar era by that designer in your wardrobe, check to see if the quality is consistent across those items.
* Many vintage designer pieces have their factories on their care labels, some common examples include Fuzzi or Aeffe.
* There aren't many counterfeit vintage goods out there, mostly because the industry boomed in the 2000s, alongside the rise of e-commerce. The confusion arises when shopping for items

that have a vintage aesthetic – for example, contemporary Chanel costume jewellery often mimics past decade fashion. However, simple things like its condition and looking online for what season it belongs to can quickly clear that up. Always give the serial number a quick search but don't be alarmed if you don't spot one or it retrieves no results. Sometimes this is because that item isn't so popular that it's all over resale sites. If you can't find one, it could have simply rubbed off over time. Serial numbers are more useful in the case of handbags to help date them and find pictures of other pieces online to serve as a point of reference.

✦ Don't be put off by what you might consider inferior quality. The techniques and innovations that we enjoy in products today didn't always exist back then. However, if the problem is glaringly obvious, such as irregular and large stitching or if the bag is made with a faux leather when the original wasn't, it's a telltale sign that it's not real.

✦ Sizing can be very misleading when it comes to vintage in that it's not a direct translation to the measurements we understand today. Most secondhand resellers, not just those dealing in vintage luxury, should be happy to provide the measurements because of this.

Ultimately, everyone wants to spend less because, why wouldn't you? But the focus shouldn't be on price. It would be far more productive to base shopping decisions on a garment's *value*, wherever you prefer to shop because this actually makes your money stretch further. It's the antidote to finding that you have nothing to wear every time you need to leave the house. And interestingly, I've found that the biggest, permanent turn-off for clothing (which means you won't be tempted to save up for something that's disappointing) is realising that it's not made well. The only thing worse than spending more than you wanted to is spending money on something that's not worth it.

As I've stated before, I don't believe most of us know how to shop. And when we don't know how to shop, prioritising low prices can mean heading to fast-fashion stores. But when we understand our fashion goals, we know what our wardrobe could benefit from and we understand the link between our finances and our mental health an entire new world opens to us. We can rent, we can even borrow from our friends or uncover unique items secondhand. All of which means spending less money better, without ever darkening the door of a fast-fashion brand.

Summary

✦ Figuring out your shopping goal is essential in learning what advice to focus on and to not get overwhelmed.

✦ Shopping goals can help you on your journey of improving your spending habits as you align the ways you consume to what matters most to you.

✦ Overconsumption is a problem most concentrated in middle-to-upper income level households; when we critique fast fashion, we are not commenting on those who most benefit from accessible price points.

✦ Donating clothes should not be our default solution. After a few wardrobe audits, the amount that is donated should dramatically reduce as you learn to shop better for long-term results.

✦ Secondhand fashion is a great resource to those who aim to be more sustainable but find themselves in need of buying something 'new'. But be cautious not to overconsume as it's not inherently sustainable just because it's preloved.

✦ Rental fashion has pros and cons but its negative aspects reflect the same of the wider fashion industry – it's not necessarily causing problems that didn't exist before.

Chapter 4

So what fabric is the most sustainable?

Since we've started a tradition of busting a myth in every chapter, here's another one: there is no such thing as sustainable materials. Yes, even natural fabrics, recycled textiles and plant-based leathers are included in that statement too. Anything else you've heard is misinformation. One of the pitfalls of misunderstanding the natural clothing argument is similar to the one that we see with the rise of thrifting – the belief that we can continue our shopping habits because the purchases are 'not as bad'.

Yvon Chouinard is the founder of Patagonia. He writes in *Let My People Go Surfing*, which he describes as a manual for employees, that 'at our present rate of consumption, we can no longer clothe the world with natural fibres'. Although he argues that natural is the more sustainable option over any synthetic substitute, it sends a clear message that shoppers simply need to buy less. Learning about the basics of clothes – the fabric with which they're made and how this is derived can really help in encouraging us to do just that.

GREEN	AMBER	RED
Recycled natural	Natural	Viscose
Cotton	Cotton	Acetate/Triacetate
Wool	Linen	Synthetic
Cashmere	Silk	Polyester
	Wool including	Acrylic
Ethical	Cashmere	Polyamide/Nylon
Silk	Vicuña, Alpaca	Polyurethane
RWS wool	Ramie	Elastane/Spandex
Good Cashmere	Hemp	
Standard	LWG leather	
Organic	Semi-synthetic	
Cotton – Global	Lyocell/TENCEL	
Organic	EcoVero/FSC	
Textile Standard,	certified	
Better	Viscose/Cupro	
Cotton initiative	Model	
Linen	Roica V50° (elastane)	
Hemp	Econyl	

Application specific but otherwise amber or red:

Plant based leather

Recycled synthetic

Repreve – recycled plastic bottles to create polyamide

Recycled polyester

Natural fibres first

When it comes to everyday clothing, there are very few exceptions to why it would need synthetic or even semi-synthetic fibres. But this doesn't mean that natural materials don't have downsides. A less-talked about issue regarding all fabrics, man-made or not, is microfibre shedding, which is often referred to in the context of plastics. However, these can be harmful even if they are made of cotton. The Department of Earth Sciences at the University of Toronto published a study on the environmental footprint of denim microfibres in 2020. While the study was focused specifically on lakes in Canada, it's interesting because it found that the natural fibre shedding was a significant contributor to human-caused pollution. In short, fashion will always leave a mark on ecosystems, no matter how conscious we are of what things are made of. Everything points to consuming less. The positive is that the Mindful Monday Method has very intentional reasons for prioritising natural fibres.

This is because natural fibres hit multiple points that are important to shopping less and better for yourself and the environment. Firstly, circularity – a coat made of wool, for example, is more likely to be resold at a second-hand shop than binned. Yes, this is a generalisation and of course it matters if it's entirely moth-eaten and smells of spaghetti bolognese. But if we're being sensible, on the whole, it's still more likely to retain its value than a polyester blend coat. Also, the fabric is important as if the brand was investing more money in what that piece is made from, it would hopefully cut fewer corners and that item would be likely to last longer. And if it should ever end up in a landfill, at the very least it will not leave as lasting of an impact as a plastic-based textile.

A pair of polyester trousers can take up to 200 years to biodegrade in a landfill, compared to cotton denim, which may take several months to a few years, depending on its thickness.

It's also about comfort for you, the wearer. Surely, if you like the way something feels on your body, you'll wear it more often. So even if the environment isn't a primary concern of yours, what it's made of still has an impact on the cost-per-wear element and hopefully you won't be replacing that item so soon.

'What about wool? I'm allergic!' I hear you say. You're not alone in thinking this. Every time I praise the properties of 100 per cent wool pieces, it's always flagged that there are people who find this fibre to be an irritant. With the wide ranging variety of quality of wool out there, I'm not surprised. I sometimes suffer from dermatographia and can't tolerate most rough garments. Sporting red-raw arms when you strip off is not a cute look. This has made me extra careful when I do my reviews or even shop for myself – I scrutinise the fibres for how fuzzy the texture is. All fabrics can pill and it's more noticeable when it comes to knitwear. But on the shop floor, we should see smoothness and no bobbling. There are exceptions – for example, some wool such as mohair that has a fine, cloud-like fluff and is used for this aesthetically desirable texture. Although, realistically, if you do find most knitwear hard to tolerate, the thought of even brushing against a fluffy cardigan like that will give you goosebumps. The reason we examine the texture of a new woollen knit is because the fuzz could be an indication that the fibres are short in length and therefore more likely to rub against the skin and itch. The irritation really comes from the friction of the fibre against skin.

A 2019 study entitled *Textile Contact Dermatitis: How Fabrics Can Induce Dermatitis* concluded, 'To date, there is an absence of evidence to substantiate allergy to wool fibres. Furthermore, allergens associated with wool processing (e.g. chemical dyes) are present at negligible levels within modern wool garments.'[xix] It's important to remember that irritation of the skin can happen with any high-fibre diameter, so the better option would be to go for premium alternatives such as superfine and ultrafine merino wool garments.

As you can see, there are so many nuances when selecting a garment, which is why we focus on establishing our fashion goals first, before committing the properties of materials to heart, so we understand what's important to us. It's hard to keep to a programme and learn to shop better if you don't fully tailor it to your lifestyle. Only when material composition is taken in context with how well a garment is made is it possible to deduce whether or not that item is a sustainable buy.

In summary, this is why avoiding synthetic fibres and opting for natural wherever possible is one of the cornerstones of the Mindful Monday Method:

1. What happens to this fabric should it ever end up in a landfill? Natural fibres will biodegrade faster,

so they're not always 'sustainable' but here's hoping they leave a lesser impact.

2. Comfort is essential to wanting to wear your clothes more often. It's important not just from a cost perspective but in terms of making it work for you, so you don't feel the need to replace it. Natural fibres are breathable and, depending on their quality, highly durable too. There are claims that silk and cotton are hypoallergenic and even antibacterial but again, depending on how it's treated in terms of dyes and processing, this may not be entirely accurate. Nevertheless, when it comes to fabrics that feel better on your skin, natural is best.

3. How much does it cost? Price is a tricky topic to navigate and not just because everyone has different tolerances. When we talk about cost in relation to garments, it's how much it was to manufacture. Driving down the price of this is essential for all brands to make a larger profit. The art is in the balance between quality and retail price. Natural fibres on the whole are more expensive to use than synthetic. That is a generalisation and cannot be applied across every article of clothing but it's a commercial consideration that brands have when designing – how much value do we want to impart to the customer?

Cotton

Origin: This is a fibre derived from the cotton plant.

Properties: Breathable, moisture absorbent, prone to shrinking, sensitive to colour – easy to dye but also easy to stain. No stretch.

Common application: This is one of the most versatile fibres and is used alone or in a blend. It can be used to create a range of weaves, such as cotton sateen, voile (a gauze-like fabric) and poplin. Cotton can be made into knitwear and even trench coats. Most commonly, it's seen in basics like t-shirts, shirts and underwear.

How is it made?: The cotton plant requires a lot of irrigation, which has earned it the nickname 'thirsty crop'. It produces a fluffy cotton 'boll' that are harvested and then spun into a fibre.

What is the quality version?: Good-quality cotton depends on the weight of the fabric, measured in gsm, which affects its transparency. Also important is the length of the fibres. Long fibres are also known as extra-long staples (ESL). These are desirable and have a pleasant, softer and smooth handfeel. When shopping for cotton basics, I always use the 'hand test': run your hand underneath the material to see if you're able to see your fingers through the fabric. The sheerness is a quick way to determine the thickness of the piece. If it's a heavily dyed garment, holding it up to the light and seeing how much filters through can give you a similar idea. When you see the terms 'Supima' (USA), 'Giza' (Egypt) and 'Sea Island' (Caribbean), this can indicate high-quality cotton.

Linen

Origin: Linen comes from the flax plant.

Properties: Naturally a light, neutral hue. Moisture absorbent, prone to creasing and breathable. No stretch.

Common application: Frequently used for summer clothing due to its cooling properties.

How is it made?: Linen is made by breaking up the stalks and leaves of the flax plant and using the inner fibres of the stalk. This is combed into thin strands that are spun into yarn.

What is the quality version?: A fabric that is soft to touch and not sheer, unless this is the desired aesthetic, in which case the handfeel is an important differentiator between an intentional look and lesser-quality linen. A tight weave is desirable, as linen can look naturally 'holey', but a smooth, compact surface is a sign of quality. Slubs are sometimes intended with linen garments, but this can also indicate that the diameter of the fibre is inconsistent and therefore not as great quality. A slub is the appearance of 'knots' in the textile.

Silk

Origin: Spun from silk worm cocoons (non-vegan).

Properties: Breathable, luxurious, drapes easily, easy to dye, versatile in appearance.

Common application: Lining for high-end fashion, occasionwear, wedding attire, pyjamas, blouses, skirts and dresses. You name it, this material has been around for thousands of years.

How is it made?: Silkworms are boiled alive (though for ethical silk, known as peace silk, cocoons are collected after the moths have hatched).

What is the quality version?: Silk can vary so weight as measured in gsm is important as this influences the sheerness. Because there are so many different applications for silk, handfeel is significant in discerning quality and can vary across the types. Charmeuse (also known as silk satin, the appearance that most people are familiar with when they think of silk) should be soft and thick; chiffon is gauzy and translucent but drapes well; crêpe de Chine is floaty with a pebbly appearance; Georgette is a plain weave that's soft to touch and organza is translucent and crisp in structure but not scratchy.

Hemp

Origin: It's derived from the plant *Cannabis sativa.*

Properties: A very strong and long fibre, there are claims that it's eight times stronger than cotton, it doesn't weaken when wet. Breathable, durable and prone to creasing.

Common application: Basics and summer clothing.

How is it made?: Hemp is heralded as a sustainable fibre as it grows incredibly fast and can be planted in a diverse range of climates. The fibre needs to be extracted from the tough outer layer of the stalk through 'retting', which is the process of allowing the stems to rot naturally in the fields or placing them in water tanks with chemicals and enzymes to speed up the process. Decortication is the process by which the core is separated from the fibres, which are then spun into a yarn. It's considered one of the most sustainable fibres available as reportedly one hectare of hemp can absorb 22 tonnes of CO_2.

What is the quality version?: Hemp has a similar appearance to flax, except the fibres are much longer. Compared to other natural materials, it can feel rougher so a soft-to-touch textile is more refined in quality.

Ramie

Origin: Ramie is the name of the plant that belongs to the nettle family, from which this material comes from.

Properties: Breathable, costly (although subject to supply and demand), resistant to high temperatures and one of the strongest natural fibres available, though hard to process for manufacturing. However, it's also quite brittle so tends to be blended with other fabrics.

Common application: An alternative to linen or silk.

How is it made?: Similar to the process of manufacturing hemp, decortication separates fibre from the bark and strips away the adhesive gum. It's labour intensive and requires heating, scraping and use of high temperatures to get rid of the natural stickiness of the plant. The time-consuming process contributes to how expensive it is. The fibres are then spun into a yarn, but as it's inflexible and breaks easily, it's difficult to do this.

What is the quality version?: Ramie is expensive to produce and isn't widely available in the mass market. Quality versions will be soft to touch with a lustre.

Wools

How is it made?: There are different processes required for each wool type, although there's a general sequence that's followed to get it to the point where it becomes yarn: shearing the animal, sorting and cleaning the wool, and carding or combing the wool to align and further clean the fibres. Carding is where the fibres are processed through wire teeth and spread out so that broken fibres and impurities can be removed. Then this is turned into a sliver that is turned into woollen thread, which can be single or multi-plied yarn. The number of plies (in other words, twists) on a staple (the technical term for the length of a fibre) goes from one to eight, from fine to bulky. Combing is mostly used for worsted threads that can be characterised by long fibres, which are smoother and more lustrous. Following either of these techniques comes spinning the wool into yarn.

What is the quality version?: As a rule of thumb, all fabrics can pill but it's more visible in knitwear because of the nature of the yarn and the variation in hair length. In the Mindful Monday Method, we pay attention to how 'fuzzy' the garment is as a quick, first sign to help tell whether or not the fibres used are higher quality. Wool of all types is often blended with other fibres, such as other wools, cotton, silk and – as more commonly seen in mass market brands – synthetic alternatives. The reason for this can be to make the product more commercially profitable for the brand by reducing its cost and/or to improve the texture and feel of the knitwear.

Take a look at the differences between the sources of various types of wool below.

Cashmere

Origin: Kashmir goats, mainly from northern India, Pakistan, Afghanistan, China and Scotland.
Properties: Recognised for its extreme softness, it's breathable, warm and lighter than sheep's wool.
Common application: Knitwear, as a single fibre or blended with less expensive ones.
How is it made?: Kashmir goats are sheared and the guard coat is separated from the undercoat – which is where cashmere is derived from. The quality of hair can be affected by the climate. There are certain restrictions for what can be called cashmere, which is influenced by the diameter of hair. The maximum allowed to have this name is ≤ 19 microns. Not to

get too geeky about cashmere but studies show that male goats produce a greater variation in the diameter and length of their undercoat hairs, meaning that the quality is generally lower than a female goat. That's your random animal fact for the day. In practice, there is really no telling what sex the goat is once you're wearing that jumper.

The ethical certification to look for is Global Recycling Standard Certified for recycled cashmere or Good Cashmere Standard.

What is the quality version?: Loro Piana is a name commonly associated with the finest cashmere. The LVMH-owned company claims to be the largest manufacturer of it. One of its two divisions is responsible for the processing of raw material and the other is a luxury fashion brand. It sources its cashmere from Mongolia and it has a reputation for being durable, using the longest and finest hairs. Loro Piana are also known for 'baby cashmere', which has extremely fine microns at 13.5 and is therefore superior in softness. Brunello Cucinelli is also cited as a brand that uses high-quality cashmere, as is Kiton (mainly known for its menswear) and Barrie, a Scottish mill that produces for Chanel. Johnstons of Elgin is another well-known brand that also does private-label production for other luxury names, although it's discreet about who the clients are – industry insiders say Burberry and Hermès are among them. Like Loro Piana, its cashmere production is 'vertically integrated', meaning that it processes the raw material in-house. Outside of brands, boiled cashmere is a term that is associated with quality. It has a dense and felted texture and is more resistant to pilling.

Vicuña

Origin: Vicuñas are members of the camel family and they're native to the Andes mountains in South America. They were listed as endangered as a result of overhunting for their wool, which has since made unregulated trade illegal.[xx] Since the 1980's, the Peruvian government gave rights to communities to shear under the National Plan for the Utilization of Vicuña. This incentivised the protection of the animals as a live vicuña came to be worth five times the value of a poached one. Hair is naturally cinnamon in colour and obtained from the neck, back, head and sides of the body. A single vicuña produces a tiny 0.5 kilograms of wool annually, which contributes to the fibre being very rare. Along with cashmere, mohair and alpaca, vicuña fibres make up 1% of the world's market share.

Properties: Notably softer than cashmere, durable and warm. And extremely expensive – multiple sources say that per kilogram of wool, it can cost a few hundred US dollars – between $399 and $600 per kg, compared to cashmere which is around $75-85 per kilo.[xxi]

Common application: A very small amount of luxury goods, such as scarves and knitwear, are produced using vicuña wool. Loro Piana is a company often associated with selling garments that are 100% vicuña, due to their major stake in the breeding and conservation of the animal.

How is it made?: Wild vicuñas are sheared every two to three years. They are fragile creatures that are sensitive to stress, so obtaining their wool is a laborious and delicate process undertaken by professionals. After the wool is sheared, it's de-haired to remove any dirt and knots. Then it's combed through to achieve a fine texture by removing shorter or broken staples. The hairs are then spun into yarn. Much of this later stage of processing is done in Italy.

CITES (Convention on International Trade in Endangered Species of Wild Fauna and Flora) is a government organisation that oversees its trade. It works with Loro Piana for the sustainable management of the animal. The LVMH-owned company has invested in conservation efforts since the 1980's which awarded them an exclusive contract to buy and sell the wool for 10 years, from 1994 to 2004. In 2008, it opened a private nature reserve which looks to protect the camelid and its habitat, to prevent overgrazing and conservation of its numbers. One of its agendas is to market the wool as a 'sustainable alternative'.[xxii]

What is the quality version?: Vicuña wool is highly prized and shearing involves a state-regulated conservation programme. Not many brands sell this and sometimes when they do, it can be found blended with other fibres. Some of these include Loro Piana and Ermenegildo Zegna. At 11-13.5 microns, which is extremely fine and soft, plus the highly monitored and limited production, it's difficult to say what is 'bad' and 'good' quality for this type of wool.

Merino wool

Origin: Merino sheep, mostly from Australia, which accounts for around 70 per cent of the world's supply.[xxiii]

Properties: Moisture wicking, warm and soft, it's also one of the most elastic natural fibres. Prone to shrinking but biodegradable, and it is also absorbent.

Common application: Knitwear, base layers, thermals, outerwear.

How is it made?: Collecting merino wool involves the usual process, except mulesing is particularly common here. This is when the flesh and wool of sheeps' buttocks are cut off, often without pain management, in order to prevent flystrike. This is when maggots bury under the animal's skin. Chemicals can be used to clean the wool to remove its natural grease. Bleach may be used to whiten wool.

What is the quality version?: Woollen fabric is usually made of shorter staples, so it is not as smooth or soft to touch. In comparison, worsted fabric has substantially longer staples with a smaller diameter (finer hairs). Its appearance is smooth. The size and length of a wool fibre determines the quality. As a gauge, merino wool is considered one of the finest at under 26 microns in diameter (comparatively, cashmere is maximum 19).

Mohair

Origin: Angora goat, mainly based in South Africa, Turkey, USA and Argentina.

Properties: Soft, durable and naturally lustrous as it has large scales on its hairs. High elasticity and easily dyed.

Common application: Knitwear, but usually blended with other fibres.

How is it made?: These goats are typically sheared twice a year. The wool is sorted according to its diameter, where it's graded between kid, young goat and adult. It then goes through the typical steps for processing wool.

What is the quality version?: Younger goats produce longer, thinner and softer wool. Kid mohair is less than 25 microns in diameter. Adult mohair is over 30 microns and is used for luxe textiles like rugs or upholstery fabric. It's rare to find a 100% mohair product on the market today, due to its high cost and so it's difficult to determine what a high quality version would be. Look for garments that are completely natural with a tight twist in the yarns and without pilling.

Alpaca

Origin: Alpacas are native to Andean highlands of Peru, Bolivia and Chile, but can be found all over the world.

Properties: Lightweight, very soft, warm, breathable, fine fibres that come in a range of natural colours from shades of white to grey and brown.

Common application: Knitwear and outerwear.

How is it made?: Alpacas are shorn once a year in the spring. Dirt and matts in the fur are cleaned and removed before shearing. After the wool is cut, it's graded by how fine it is. It's then cleaned again and spun into yarn, ready to make into a garment. Responsible Wool Standard is a good choice when shopping for alpaca; one of its guarantees is that the animal is 'allowed to behave naturally and not be subjected to practices that cause them stress or discomfort'.

What is the quality version?: There are two types of alpaca. Huacaya, whose wool is fluffy with fibres below 20 microns in diameter and is the most valuable. Then there's the suri breed, which has longer hairs with high lustre. Its quality is also based on how uniform the length of the staples are.

Leather

Origin: Animal hide. The most common leathers that we see on the market are cow, calf, sheep and lamb.

Properties: Durable, water resistant, ages well and natural insulator. Different leathers vary in suppleness, grain (the texture on the surface of the skin) and strength.

Common application: Accessories such as wallets, gloves, shoes and bags, and a variety of garments.

How is it made?: Skin is dehaired and cleaned. If the skin is inconsistent in thickness, it may be split to make it more uniform. Chemical tanning or vegetable tanning takes place. The first uses a chromium salt solution. As it is absorbed, it crosslinks the proteins to make the leather water-resistant. The second involves soaking the hide in concentrated 'natural' tannins derived from plant materials, such as bark, leaves and fruits. After the leather is tanned, it's dyed. Look for Leather Working Group certifications, which looks at the environmental impact of every stage of leather production to ensure sustainable and responsible practices. These involve traceability and transparency, chemical management to limit the use of hazardous materials (like chromium salts). and ensuring safe working conditions. LWG awards tanneries and factories with different grades: 'Audited', which means the supplier hasn't reached the minimum requirement for certification; Bronze, signifying basic requirements are met; Silver shows a 'good' level of compliance and Gold means the highest level of commitment to the LWG standards.

What is the quality version?: Leather is a natural product prone to imperfections and variations in its thickness. 'Full skins' – larger sections of skins – is a point of pride for retailers, who want to show that the leather used is high quality. This means that some brands, depending on the product, will opt for designs where you'll see fewer pieces stitched together, to prioritise the natural beauty of the skin. However, this can vary greatly depending on the design aesthetic and product. It's perhaps more useful to think about whether the surface is heavily treated – an indication of this is if it creases and scratches easily. If it smells earthy and 'natural' and retains its suppleness, it's likely to have received less coating (which is plastic based and can make the leather appear more expensive by looking uniform, without it being the best quality). This is also an area where the purpose of using leather matters. For example, a strap of a shoe that's made of lambskin or sheepskin is going to cause less friction on the skin. It's a softer leather than cow's and possibly the more expensive option.

Leather is often marketed as the by-product of the food waste industry. Critics of this argue that by-product is a waste material and the skin of an animal is more valuable than its meat, therefore animals are raised for their hide. The industrialisation of cattle farming is not a sustainable endeavour, no matter what the purpose. It has contributed to deforestation, so brands conscious of this that prefer the natural textile instead of its plant- and plastic-based counterparts may choose to avoid ranches near the Amazon rainforest, for example. Cattle also generate a lot of methane emissions – a greenhouse gas – and produce a lot of waste. This is even before discussing the toxic chemicals, like chromium, associated with chrome-tanned leather, formaldehyde, as well as heavy metals like lead and mercury that are health risks to those working with it. We will discuss leather in depth later on in this chapter.

Rayon and co.

Origin: 'Rayon' refers to a cellulose based material, often derived from wood pulp that is chemically processed to create fibres that can then be spun into yarn. Modal is derived from the beech tree, which is considered to be a lower impact source because it uses less irrigation and recycles the water and chemicals used. Cupro uses cotton linter, the waste product of cotton production. Lyocell is a more circular form of viscose and has a 'closed-loop' manufacturing process. The branded version, named TENCEL and created by Lenzing AG, claims to be able to reuse 99 per cent of the solvent it uses.

Properties: Smooth, silky, absorbent but very weak when wet. It shrinks easily and can be difficult to launder.

Common application: Everyday garments and occasion-wear. It can be adapted to several looks; for example, it's often known as vegan silk because it can mimic the appearance of silk satin. It's slightly different to the natural and synthetic fibres because this is a mix of both. The good news is that it's biodegradable, meaning that it can hypothetically be broken down in soil by microorganisms.

What is the quality version?: The rayon family is a big one where everyone kind of looks the same and they have similar properties. There is a prolific use of viscose in mass fashion collections as it is cheaper than silk but mimics the appearance very well. The difference in quality can be determined by handfeel. How soft, thick and smooth is the textile? Poor-quality viscose can sometimes feel rough and start to pill so quickly that it may even be visible on new clothing in stores. It can also snag easily. Similar to the concept of wool, the length of the fibres affects the final material. Mercerisation is a chemical process which is sometimes used as it strengthens a fabric and creates a lustre (this isn't exclusive to viscose, it can be applied to cotton too). It's debatable how sustainable it is as this step involves further water use and sodium hydroxide. This chemical is caustic and if not properly handled can contaminate water supplies, altering its pH and killing aquatic life. However, this can improve the appearance and touch of the fabric, which is why it's utilised.

Synthetics

There's a tendency to oversimplify things in a culture where quick-to-digest information is the most attractive. In a lot of my reviews, I slate the use of synthetics in clothing because it's excessive. It's cheap and fossil-fuel based, meaning that it takes extensive resources to create these materials, as well as wreaking havoc on the environment in its post-consumer journey. Although, not all synthetics are bad. We need to be reasonable! Some garments require technical fabrics that need to be plastic-based – for example, waterproofs, swimwear and high visibility items that are essential for workplace safety. I also make an exception for occasionwear, but not the kind of body socks you see on fast-fashion websites being sold off for £1 on Black Friday. I mean designs with a point of view. If we're to accept that designers are textile artists of sorts, the medium in which they choose to express their visions may not always be of natural origin.

Amidst these, you'll notice that there are extremely few exceptions made for everyday clothing.

In 2000, polyester overtook cotton as the most used material in garments. It's important to note that there are expensive, even luxurious, versions of polyester. With any fabric, there are different qualities available, but due to how cheap polyester can get, the most common examples we see are on the lower end of the quality scale (a quick search for wholesale polyester fabric on Alibaba, a Chinese wholesale online marketplace, will show you many results starting at 0.55 cents per metre). It's especially worrying when, according to a McKinsey report, the average consumer purchased 60 per cent more clothing in 2014 than in 2000. The two data points make perfect sense. Polyester is generally less expensive to use than cotton and more forgiving. This is because polyester affords a great deal of stretch if it's in a knit form, which alleviates the need for detailed patterns to ensure a good fit. Therefore, if we keep pulling on this thread we can see that a garment is designed to be cheap and avoid basic dressmaking needs like fitting. Planned obsolescence is at play. The result is a dissatisfied customer that doesn't understand why, places the onus on themselves and keeps buying more because they don't realise that it's the retailer that's causing these issues.

Then there are the microplastics. PET is the main plastic used for polyester and the Ellen MacArthur Foundation estimates that these fibres make up around 60 per cent of all clothing, although this may also include blends. We know that all materials can shed microfibres, but the ones that we might find most concerning are the plastic variety. Bioaccumulation is one of the reasons why – this is when plastic particles end up in the food chain as animals consume this, which eventually ends up in our bodies.

Tips on how to limit microplastic shedding:

* If you're able to foot the extra cost, installing a microfibre filter to your washing machine could help reduce water pollution from the shedding associated with frequent and small wash loads.
* Wash with full loads as that limits the amount of friction in the washing machine, which encourages fibre shedding.
* Try to limit buying synthetic fibres wherever possible! Depending on your fashion goals, this could even extend to secondhand goods.
* Handwash or spotwash wherever possible as most clothes don't need to be laundered after every wear.

Polyester

Origin: Polyester is a man-made synthetic fibre that was made commercially viable in the 1940s. It grew in popularity following the Second World War when natural fibres were in short supply. In 1956, the American company DuPont bought the production rights and named the textile Dacron.

Properties: Relatively cheap, it holds its shape, is durable, moisture-wicking, versatile – for example, can be used as a knit (the yarns look like they're looped) or a woven fabric (the yarns are criss-crossed).

Common application: In the early 2000s, polyester overtook cotton as the most commonly used fibre as it became more economical. It's found in an array of clothing and often seen blended with natural materials. This can reduce the cost of using a 100% natural textile but it also lends its properties.

How is it made?: Ethylene glycol is a chemical compound derived from petroleum (fossil fuels) and comes in liquid form. Terephthalic acid (which comes from crude oil) is a white, crystalline substance. They react together in a process called polymerisation, which produces long polymer chains. These are spun into fibres that are used to make polyester fabric.

What is the quality version?: Good-quality polyester very much exists, even though it's associated with cheap fast fashion. Its quality is somewhat dependent on its potential to fulfil its purpose. For example, retaining vivid colour that lasts after multiple washes and lasting a long time, which is in part due to its tenacity (strength). An easy way to think about this it is how resistant the fabric is to wear and tear, and this is measured in grams per denier or g/d. Polyester clothing uses a range between 4.5 to 6.5 g/d, but using much higher than this isn't always desirable because this is the sort of fabric you'd associate with industrial textiles.

Acrylic

Origin: A crude oil-derived polymer called polyacrylonitrile (PAN).

Properties: Resistant to moths, durable and has a soft handfeel.

Common application: Acrylic is often used as a cheaper substitute for wool fibres. See common application for wool.

How is it made?: A polymer solution using PAN and other chemicals, such as acrylonitrile (a toxic and flammable liquid classified as a carcinogen but its threat is mostly contained to exposure in the manufacturing process), is used. This is heated and pressurised, which creates a polymer. The polymer is pumped through a spinneret to create long, thin fibres that are stretched out through a process called 'drawing'. This makes the fibre more uniform and extends the length and tension for the sake of durability and strength. The acrylic fibres are crimped to create a texture similar to natural wool. The spiral shape also creates the appearance of volume.

What is the quality version?: Quality acrylic is very

soft, doesn't transfer colour and will not look like it's pilling prematurely (on new clothes, there should be no excessive fuzz or bobbling). It should have good resistance to laundering.

Polyamide/nylon

Origin: Polyamide was first made by the DuPont Corporation in the early 1920s but took off post-war as an alternative to cotton and silk that were in short supply. The term 'polyamide' refers to a polymer with repeating amino acids. Some people may be confused as silk, derived from silkworm cocoons, is technically also a polyamide. However, when we use this term we are referring to nylon.

Properties: Stretchy, water resistant, lightweight and durable.

Common application: Sportswear and blends to provide stretch. Hosiery, swimwear and waterproof garments.

How is it made?: The polymer is made from a reaction between a diamine and a dicarboxylic acid. The most common ones used in its production are adipic acid and hexamethylenediamine (HMDA). Adipic acid is a white crystalline powder and HMDA is a liquid compound. Both usually come from crude oil production. The reaction results in the formation of nylon 66, which is named after the number of carbon atoms in its monomers. This monomer is fed through a spinneret, which creates the fibres.

What is the quality version?: Nylon is often blended with other fabrics, so discerning its quality can be difficult in this context. However, it's especially well exhibited in quality sportswear. It should have a good four-way stretch and recovery, meaning that it's able to stretch in all directions. Denier is the measurement of the weight of a single strand of fibre. A higher denier corresponds to tighter, denser look that can add to its resistance to tearing. In the case of nylon, we often see this in hosiery where the larger the number the thicker the tights.

Polyurethane

Origin: Polyurethane is formed by a reaction between a polyol with a diisocyanate. The source of the polyol is often from fossil fuel production, but doesn't have to be, for example, some polyols are derived from vegetable oil.

Properties: Water resistant and easy to clean, with a smooth texture.

Common application: Polyurethane is often used to make PU, which has been marketed as 'vegan leather', faux leather or pleather. It can also be applied as a coating to garments to make them waterproof and shiny.

How is it made?: The polyol and diisocyanate is reacted together with heat and catalysts are added to control this. Additives are included to enhance desirable properties, such as being flame retardant and UV resistant. It's then coated onto a base fabric such as polyester and nylon, although cotton may also be used. When this is dried, it would be considered a polyurethane material. Depending on its use, it can be embossed to mimic the grain on leather or laminated for a shine.

What is the quality version?: Good PU should not peel or crack easily. As it's technically a coating, it should be flexible and not separate from its base. There should also be no bubbling and it should repel water.

Next generation materials and luxury brands

This is a good time to talk about one of the most interesting scientific developments in the sustainability space: the performance and environmental impact of 'alternative leathers'. So far, companies have created 'leather' from cactus, grape, pineapple, corn, fungi and even orange peel. The Material Innovation Initiative is a non-profit that researches the possibilities of next generation materials. The organisation reported that since 2015, $2.3 billion USD has been invested in developing non-animal based textiles. A significant boom happened in 2021, when $980 million was raised, double what was generated in the previous year. Some particularly high-profile applications have incited a lot of buzz over the value of these new materials and whether they are even a desirable alternative in the luxury space. In 2021, Hermès announced a new bag called Victoria, made of bio-textile with the brand name Sylvania, derived from Fine Mycelium™, from MycoWorks. This is a made-to-order material that can be fully customised in thickness, length, size and flexibility – a benefit of using fungus as the base material as opposed to other cellulose. Can it compete with the quality of leather that Hermès is known for or is that not the point?

Luxury has historically been slow to accept that sustainability is an essential part of the business of fashion. And the designer brands that do make eco claims often use floral language that sounds more like a Gwyneth Paltrow soundbite than anything with purpose. They've also been quick to defer to the idea that their products are of such high quality and retain so much value that this is already sustainable, in and of itself. The Mindful Monday Method places high standards of clothing quality as the crux of a sustainable buy, so you might think I support this. I don't.

At the risk of sounding cynical, brands that are hoping to align their name and reputation with the latest innovations in materials may have motivations beyond being truly environmentally minded. Putting money where your mouth is significant and it's a sizable investment to co-create, such as the case with Hermès. Smaller premium brands that position themselves as sustainable fashion leaders have also adopted alternative leathers, like GANNI and Pangaia. At the crux of it, being one of the first to use a material that everyone is curious about is a fantastic marketing tool.

The long-term pay-off is that if new generation materials in fashion become widely adopted, the brands that have invested in it are the frontrunners of the movement. It's not just a brand building exercise but an investment in its financial future. Sustainability wise, it's easier to talk about how exciting a new material is than address trickier questions over waste management, supply chains and overproduction.

At present, and for the foreseeable future, Sylvia, the reishi-based bio leather, is exclusive to Hermès. This means that they have an enormous degree of control over an entire textile type. We might presume it's the highest quality non-animal leather (thanks to brand association), but you'll have to wait for your sales assistant to WhatsApp you about its availability, just as if you're looking for a coveted bag. It comes down to exclusivity, which breeds hype, which raises prices.

It's pretty normal for maisons to pursue supply chain integration by buying up production sites. It's an old strategy spun in an earth-conscious way. For example, in 2012, Chanel bought Scottish cashmere house Barrie. A year later, it purchased the Bodin Joyeux tannery and, in 2016, a majority stake in Megisserie Richard, a sheep leather tannery, to secure their supply. Assimilating coveted, high-quality suppliers doesn't just ensure that a luxury brand has enough to sell to its awaiting loyalists, it also means your competitors have a little less access too. It's all about the money. Any time you're confused about something in the fashion industry, start with the cash and work backwards until you find your answer.

I spoke to Paolo de Cesare, a CEO well versed in the strategies of luxury brands, about why sustainability has taken a back seat for so long and why it seems like a side note. He answered by asking me to think of the largest brands in the world. If we look at the most recent revenue figures published (2022), Louis Vuitton brought in 20 billion euros for LVMH, Chanel 15.6 billion and Christian Dior 79.2 billion. 'Do you associate these brands with sustain-ability? Is the primary promise or primary reason for buying, sustainability? Not at all. If they were perceived as bad for sustainability, it will be an issue. I think sustainability is a must-have. But it's not yet a differentiator that can distort the performance of a brand.'

Stella McCartney is a luxury fashion brand that's synonymous with never using real leather. The cost of its faux-leather pieces matches that of real leather accessories from competitors. The world first saw the label's Mylo baby on the runway for Spring/Summer 2022 – a handbag crafted from the fungi-based textile mycelium, created by Bolt Threads. Featuring a signature chain, it goes for over £1,000. Just a few years on, in 2023, Bolt Threads CEO Dan Widmaier announced that the mushroom based textile would cease production. The reason being a decrease in funding opportunities to raise manufacturing to a commercial scale. Sustainable endeavours are a highly expensive undertaking. Perhaps some see it as rightly so, as penance for past wrongdoings against the planet. I take this as a reminder that it's easy to stand as an outsider and criticise. It is significantly much harder to be a player in the arena believing in a mission, coming so close but missing the mark.

OK, but is it worth it?

Aside from the ethical argument, which is really up to individuals to decide what they're comfortable with, the durability of alternative leather is heavily contested. At least for the first iterations that we're seeing on the market. Desserto, a textile made of nopal cactus, which is chosen for its ability to grow in arid conditions, without taking away from other crops. However, it's non-recyclable, contains plastic and therefore isn't biodegradable. Piñatex may be derived from pineapple leaves and its waste can be repurposed for feedstock, but it contains a significant amount of polyurethane (Bio PU) and mirrors the same issue as before. For vegans, this may be a pay-off that individuals are willing to make. A little bit of plastic in exchange for guilt-free shoes is reasonable. The issue with these leather alternatives becoming a natural choice for shoppers is that they are not yet the answer we expected them to be.

This is exactly where having a fashion goal comes in useful because this isn't going to be the case for everyone. For example, if you are someone who would buy less but buy better and not vegan, the easy answer is to invest in high-quality genuine leather goods. I mean genuine as in real. Not the dubious 'genuine leather' that can also be coated in plastic. And if your fashion goal is to avoid shopping new as much as possible, then opting for a vintage leather jacket would be preferable.

Piñatexe Performance Pineapple Leather

Product Details

✎ Dimensions

📋 **Technical Details**

- Contains 46% Pineapple Leaf Fibre (PALF); 36% PU; 12% Polylactic Acid (OLA); 6% Bio PU
- Tensile Strength (along): 816 N
- Tensile Strength (across): 701 N
- Tear Strength (along): 210 N
- Tear Strength (across): 163 N
- Softness: 2.10 mm
- Density: 0.223 g/cm3
- Grammage: 567 g/m
- Finish Adhesion: >10N/10mm

This is the composition of Piñatex, a new innovation of using pineapples to create textile. The significant 36% is PU, which refers to polyurethane. The lack of 'bio' denotes that this is likely to be fossil fuel derived. There is also 6% Bio PU, which suggests a minority uses a plant-based source for the polyol.

A few years ago, I bought a pair of trainers made of corn leather. I'd seen them advertised all over my social media feed and some of my influencer acquaintances wearing them. (Sidenote: people who have a lot of fashion items that they didn't pay for aren't the most credible when it comes to quality. Things tend to last a long time when you have so many options and don't need to wear the same thing multiple times a week.) That's not to say that there's ill intent or deception. These trainers had a vintage aesthetic and were possibly my favourite design I'd ever come across. The brand actually made them in my size (I'm a UK 2) and it was my first time seeing plant-based leather that didn't look like a plastic shell or a crumpled receipt. I'd never wanted to like anything more. I wore them every day for a month and by the end of it, they were completely falling apart. I'm talking about holes worn into the sock of the shoe, the insole coming apart and the outsole wearing down so much that it went from a flat surface to a black diamond piste. That's £100 I'll never see again.

You may think 'but it's made of veggies, it'll biodegrade!' Not quite. There are hundreds of components involved in making a sneaker, making it extremely hard to recycle anyway. The problem isn't exclusive to synthetic-based shoes – it's a category-wide concern. But the expectation was that it would last at least as long as a regular trainer, otherwise was it really necessary to make it and do we really need another footwear brand? The argument in defence is always the same: when using a relatively new innovation, there is a pay-off; you can't get everything right when you're trying to be different. This is why it's such a challenge to recommend what is marketed as 'vegan leather', which is quite an emotive term. So to strip it back and look at its benefits for the customer, simply ask 'does this align with my shopping goal?' And if the answer is no to both, you may want to rethink that purchase.

It's no wonder that defenders of leather so easily maintain their stance. Fashion designer Gabriela Hearst runs her eponymous luxury womenswear brand but is also responsible for leading Chloé to B-Corp status – the first in LVMH's portfolio to achieve this. After her Autumn/Winter 2024 show, which she calls 'her favourite' for the French luxury brand, she told UK newspaper the *Guardian*, 'For as long as we are eating meat, leather is a by-product of that.' She's not wrong, but I have to say, with fingers crossed, I'm awaiting the result of the huge investments made in the next generation of materials. I'm rooting for them because we can't go on relying on the status quo when we know how devastating the impact currently is.

Supply and demand

Should fast fashion brands be allowed in the conversation about sustainable fashion? Whatever your take on this, the largest argument for their involvement is the economics of supply and demand.

What happens is a particular material becomes popularised and adopted by huge retailers – an example of this might be Lenzing's TENCEL, the brand name for lyocell. Demand creates competition, which makes costs more competitive, so smaller brands that may not be able to achieve the same volume of orders will eventually be able to use that material too. My first encounter of this material in mainstream fashion was when it was used by

Inditex brands. A few years later, 'sustainable' businesses adopted it.

Did you know that the majority of recycled polyester clothing out there is derived from plastic bottles and not post-consumer clothing? Critics – myself included – believe that it's not quite as praiseworthy as brands like to make it out to be. Plastic bottles can create other plastic bottles, so taking from this closed loop and producing clothes that cannot be recycled again seems like a 'on a need to basis' as opposed to a sustainable option. Or did you know that recycled polyamide, which you may have heard of under the brand name Econyl, is made from the likes of discarded fishing nets? Both recycled materials are lower impact than their virgin counterparts that rely on fossil fuels to be produced. But they are only 'sustainable' when used where required. Examples might be a waterproof jacket or a swimsuit. A very promising innovation is Circulose, a cellulose-based material composed of cotton and viscose fibres created by Swedish company Renewcell. So yes, it is technically biodegradable. The key differentiator is that this creates fabric out of old clothes, which is what's truly needed when landfills are filling up, waste colonialism is rife and there is already so much textile out there.

Wait until you find out who was among the first to popularise it: Levi's. On its website, the denim retailer writes that it is, 'fully recyclable and made with recycled materials that still live up to our durability standards. Meet our first circular 501® jeans'.[xxiv] H&M group brands Weekday, H&M and COS have also incorporated Circulose in their collections. These are all brands that came under fire for not paying supply chain workers during the Covid-19 pandemic, which was highlighted by the fair wage campaign #PayUp, led by the non-profit organisation Remake. If you're confused, I don't blame you. Sustainable fashion is far from easy to navigate, which is a great time yet again to plug how important it is to understand your fashion goal and thus your priorities when you learn more about the industry!

So you've heard about the benefits of supply and demand, but not the disadvantages. As you might've guessed, it doesn't always work in the favour of the environment. One of the most rampant issues is the rise in popularity of cashmere. Once recognised as highly luxurious, the fibre that comes from the undercoat of the Kashmir goat started appearing on the high street and, eventually, on the racks of fast-fashion stores. Not all cashmere pieces are made equal, even if there are tight restrictions on what might be disclosed as such on a care label. Retailers like Uniqlo sell one of these jumpers for as low as £60. If I'm honest, the quality I've seen is really good for the price. But it's only good for our wallets and not much else. Unfortunately, the price is paid elsewhere, in animal welfare or in the cost of labour somewhere along the supply chain.

The demand for cashmere wool has contributed to the desertification of grasslands due to overgrazing goats. Shepherds have also been known to kill natural predators such as snow leopards in a bid to protect their flock. Ethical certifications like the Good Cashmere Standard can give shoppers confidence that regulations have been put in place to limit this risk. But remember that it's exactly that: a limitation. Nothing is perfect or guaranteed. I won't pretend that it's anywhere close to a bad idea to buy an affordable cashmere sweater. Especially if it's the more economical and maybe even more sustainable option than cranking up the heating and having your energy bill soar. Nor is this to say that all luxury brands use cashmere in a responsible way or that it's better to snap up all the shoddy acrylic sweaters out there. Knowledge is all part of making informed decisions and it's important to recognise the implications of having an animal product with a price tag that is constantly being driven down. As always, the moral of the story is to buy only what you need and if possible, always look to secondhand first.

Cultural versus material value

Our visual diet is the content that we consume, whether it's via social media, television or traditional advertising. Through exposure, we end up internalising what we see. It's something most of us barely pay attention to yet this has such a profound influence on our mood. Over time, it can even shape our beliefs. I call it social osmosis. A critical part of this is the push-and-pull relationship between material and cultural value.

Let's talk about material culture. I don't see this as an antidote to cultural value but rather a balancing counterpart to hype. Call it the substance to the style, if you will. One of the best examples of material culture education comes from Tanner Leatherstein, a TikTok account that asks whether a luxury item is 'worth it'. At the time of writing, it's well on its way to hitting 1,000,000 followers. The man behind the social and cultural phenomena is Volkan Yilmaz, who comes from a family of tanners and runs his own leather brand, Pegai.

Since he was ten years old, one of his hobbies has been making leather jackets for himself. He moved to the US for a consultancy job and was looking for a work bag but couldn't find leather to the quality he expected. He started dissecting designer handbags – the likes of Coach, Bottega Veneta, Louis Vuitton and LOEWE – as a result of frustration. In his viral videos, Yilmaz analyses how much leather is used and what it is. For example, the difference between genuine calfskin and bonded leather – things that most people didn't think had significant differences.

If you are wondering – and I know you are – bonded leather can barely be considered true leather at all. It's a textile made of reconstituted leather glued to a paper backing and strengthened by a polyurethane coating. Imagine paying a premium for that. If you baulked, then perhaps material value means a lot more to you than you might've thought.

The leather expert and craftsman evaluates the cost

of the hardware, the complexity of the design and how that influences the price of labour. And if you didn't think it could get more forensic, Yilmaz uses an acetone test, which takes off the top layers of finishing on the material, to discern just how heavily treated it is. This can be an indication of the quality of the material used. Then there's the ash test, which is visually gripping as he torches slices of fabric. We hold our breath, waiting to see if his leather sample will melt like plastic or char like wood. But this is not about theatrics; there's a method to madness. Yilmaz demonstrates how vegetable tanned products, which are better for the environment than chrome-tanned, will burn more like charcoal.

Visual diet is changing, undoubtedly driven by the rising economic power and distinct cultural tastes of Gen Z. Let me tell you, there is nothing more humbling than seeing the outfits you wore at 13 and cringed at when you were 18 return to pop culture when you are 30. Fashion is indeed cyclical but there has been some progress, if we look at it through the lens of sustainability.

Now more than ever before, companies are forced to focus on what values they want to convey. Ethics has become a sort of currency of coolness for brands. 'Gen Z don't really care about marketing fluff. They're more into meaning. They have a different level of consciousness that the older generations didn't have. They really want meaning in their choices rather than empty marketing stuff that doesn't really mean anything but it worked before,' Yilmaz tells me over a video call. And it's true.

According to the report 'The State of Fashion' by McKinsey, data found that Gen Z and Millennials represented $350 billion of spending power in the United States. Moreover, Gen Z will account for 40 per cent of global consumers by 2020 and are intrinsically motivated to support brands that have a clear stance on environmental and social issues that align with theirs. They're also very willing to boycott those that don't.[xxv]

We are entering an era when, finally, customers are recognising their power and demanding change. This is the collective that shamed Chanel, who the fashion industry perceived as untouchable, into temporarily closing their TikTok account. The decision came after a £825 Christmas advent calendar unboxing went viral and was condemned as a rip off. But it's also the same generation that influenced Tiffany & Co.'s pivot to embrace youth culture. The high jewellery brand tapped Blackpink's star Rosé as the face of the brand in 2021. It's this Gen Z cohort that's hugely invested in the acquisition process of a Birkin bag and has revived interest in old-school heritage brands like Loro Piana, thanks to viral videos from comedian Gustaf Lundberg Toresson, who posts under the name Gstaad Guy.

Leather is the perfect material to discuss in the realm of material value, as knowledge around its production is arguably more shrouded than soft fabrics, like shirts and trousers. There's also a degree of mystique and people assume that all leather is more or less the same in quality and can always demand a premium. However, the Tanner

Leatherstein account demonstrates the same message as the Mindful Monday Method: we must use the free knowledge that visual culture provides to become more mindful shoppers.

Let me take you back to the fourteenth and fifteenth centuries, classified in the West as the Early Renaissance. Then, the most famous paintings we know were mainly commissioned by the Church. During this period, the cost of these artworks was heavily influenced by the quality of materials used, perhaps more than the name of the artist behind it. For example, the much-coveted stone lapis lazuli for the Virgin Mary's blue cloak. Precious gold used as accents to suggest a supernatural holiness radiating from the canvas. Ask a pedestrian to name an artist from this period and it's unlikely they'll have the name Fra Angelico rolling off their tongue. Compare this to the High Renaissance period, where we immediately think of the likes of Leonardo da Vinci, Tiziano Vecellio (or Titian) and Michelangelo di Lodovico Buonarroti Simoni (also known as Michelangelo to friends and fans). There are many more that come to mind if you're an art buff. This rise was somewhat compounded by the money of patrons such as the famed Medici family.

As interest increased in who was behind the spectacular works and the masterpieces, I would argue so too did the emergence of cultural value. If we are to agree that fashion in its highest form is an arm of the art world, then to demean cultural value completely by only placing emphasis on material value is reductive. And, frankly, a little bit boring. The masters of fashion have built reputations that years on from their passing, mean that their names can command extreme prices: Yves Saint Laurent, Hubert de Givenchy and Christian Ernest Dior to name a few.

However, with the rise of digital visual culture and its 24-hour shelf life, constant whirlwind of newness and reductive commentary, cultural value has been distorted and suppressed to be frenzied and commodified. Everything has become so fast that it's not about the maker or even the product itself, but simply how it is presented. There has been a prolific rise of cult designers in recent years, their profiles accelerated by social media and being worn by celebrities. They cosplay as luxury brands. They've even had instrumental parts in shaping entire aesthetics, the way that was previously exclusive to couture houses. And so the final product, what is actually available to purchase by you and I, is overlooked by the majority of consumers, who are distracted by the beautifully orchestrated runway shows and the models with famous last names who wear the brand. It's not just about changing the font of a logo or hiring a fresh faced, mysterious designer. Understanding how to woo the internet is essential too. In 2022, Coperni generated applause and a viral fashion moment when model Bella Hadid was dressed in front of an audience with a spray-on white 'textile'. It was likened to Alexander McQueen's iconic production, in which Shalom Harlow's white dress was graffitied by robots and spray paint. But when I went to review a spring collection, I was astounded by what I saw. Of course there were a few beautiful pieces (and this is why I stress looking at items individually instead of applauding or berating an entire brand) but there was also a see-through, 100 per cent polyester bright blue dress with its overlock exposed. It didn't scream £360, to me it said 'Fast Fashion With A Gigantic Markup'.

Alec Leach is an author and the ex-fashion editor at Highsnobiety. He tells me that in the world of menswear, the surge of cultural value all began with the streetwear boom around 2014. It was the revolutionary, almost guerrilla tactics of limited drops, pop-ups and collaborations between brands with a cult following to merge their fanbase that made the executives at luxury brands sit up and pay attention. It also had a huge influence on the aesthetic of how men dress today.

The example of hype in menswear is interesting because it happened recently enough for us to track it and witness the pivot point where cultural value begins to supersede material value. As the world's largest fashion houses saw the incredible impact that the movement had on fashion and building communities, the likes of Louis Vuitton, Dior, Gucci and Ermenegildo Zegna subsequently launched collaborations with streetwear brands. The majority of us don't peruse these sites daily, but the strategies that these major fashion houses follow, still has a profound impact on how people like you and I shop. This is because cultural value trickles down. What we see on the runways is sold to us in a diffused form in high street shops. It influences the work of younger designers and becomes viral moments on social media that we see over and over again, in short clips paired with punchy, hyperfast music. Cultural value has been imbued with so much importance that every collaboration or limited edition item becomes so hot that it implodes and dissipates. In the world of womenswear, think about Fendace (the high profile capsule from Versace and Fendi) or Adidas and their slew of luxe partnerships with Gucci and Balenciaga. These items appear across social media for a few weeks before we get nauseated by seeing them everywhere. Then seemingly as fast as it was built up, the enthusiasm for these items die down. Clothes emblazoned with enormous logos shrink to the back of closets all over the world. Perhaps we'll see those pieces again on a luxury resale website in a few years' time, when the hype has been dead long enough that it'll be cool again to wear. Frankly, the cycle of fashion is ridiculous when we put so much importance on cultural value alone.

One thing that consumers are excited to take away from the Mindful Monday Method is that expensive does not equate to high quality. It's validation that it's all smoke and mirrors and no, you're not crazy for having seen that all along. The harder part is knowing where to start. It can sometimes feel like we're back at square one, a teenager with a bit of pocket money who's been let loose in a busy shopping mall, but, this time, trying to relearn how to shop through the lens of quality. This takes us onto the next chapter – understanding what makes a quality garment so that you can honour your best self through an act that we do almost every day: shopping.

Summary

✦ No material is completely sustainable.

✦ Prioritise shopping natural fibres for circularity and comfort.

✦ Not all synthetics are bad – for example, technical fabrics such as sportswear and waterproofs, and specialised garments like high-visibility vests. It may even be a better option in terms of affordability and practical use to buy a synthetic puffer coat over a thick wool one, which can be quite inaccessible.

✦ There are poor-quality materials across the natural, semi-synthetic, synthetic and new generation textiles.

✦ Materials impact the cost of a garment; it's important to factor in what your clothes are made of.

✦ Ask yourself 'If I can't take a photo in this would I still want to buy it?' which can help determine if you want an item for its cultural or material value. Are you comfortable with where your priority lies on that spectrum? Only you can determine this.

Chapter 5

Sustainable buys, not sustainable brands

Before we understand the technical side of what quality clothes look like, it's important to start with why we want to shop quality. On the surface, it's probably because we want to look good. Dig a little deeper, maybe we want to save money in the long run. Further than that, I think we really want to feel at peace with our wardrobes.

So much of the sustainable fashion conversation has been dominated by which brand to shop from. Who does the most ethical underwear? Which trainers have the lowest impact? The issue with this is that it reduces clothing to very arbitrary standards that, frankly, brands can be less open about. Shopping for quality isn't about relying on these businesses but understanding what a sustainable buy looks like, for you.

One of the challenges in this journey is that advertising has made it far more confusing by turning sustainability into an ethical minefield for consumers. This issue is compounded by the serious lack of regulation around what terminology can be used in communicating credentials. Words like 'responsible', 'sustainable' and 'conscious' are used interchangeably to all mean the same thing: 'better'.

I'd like to propose that we reframe the way we think about sustainable brands and even sustainable products.

In 2019, while I was researching articles for a magazine editor, I came across an interesting read. Especially for a pre-pandemic piece, when the sustainability conversation in fashion offices was only just beginning. It was glaringly insightful. I can't recall the publication or author now, and yes, of course I've tried to Google it. The journalist argued that instead of thinking of a 'sustainable' item as a better alternative, we should swap it for the term 'less bad' instead. Sustainable fashion is less bad than mainstream fashion. That sounds way more accurate to me.

We need to recognise that producing anything new, especially at high volumes that get shipped all around the globe, cannot truly be 'sustainable'. We also need to realise that sustainability cannot exist without being inclusive and respectful of each other. When so much production takes place in the shadows, where forced labour, unsafe working conditions and withheld salaries are the norm, how can we be so quick to accept that anything is sustainable?

On the consumer side of things, reflect on how many clothes actually cater to your body and needs. Think about how surprised you are when you find something that fits perfectly! I wonder if we'd take the same approach at the supermarket. We are not pleasantly surprised when we buy food that isn't spoiled. This relaxation of standards has come about through our utter reliance on brands, which means we've settled for less. There is nothing more revealing of this than watching a try-on haul video. Next time you're browsing YouTube, watch out for a video where something is fobbed off as 'oversized' and 'cosy' when actually, it's just ill-fitting.

Relying on brands doesn't actually make our lives easier or more beautiful. The act of owning things doesn't buy you the dream that these brands present. Between 1994 and 2004, photographer Kyoichi Tsuzuki captured 30 Japanese collectors of brands, from Paul & Joe to Gucci, surrounded by mounds of clothing in their homes. In the series of photos, entitled *Happy Victims*, the subjects are captured in an intimate setting, relaxed in their personal space. The viewer might even imagine that they've stumbled across a private image that belongs in the fold of a wallet and not a coffee table book. That is until they notice the way that the items of clothing – almost indiscernible as they are stacked on top of each other, except for a bra hanging from a balcony or the line-up of women's heels – dominates the forefront of the images. These fashion lovers aren't millionaires in sprawling, plush suites. They aren't collectors of archival Margiela, housing garments in a temperature-controlled vault. The set-up is far from an Instagram snapshot. In their small apartments, the subjects look so relatable that you might even imagine yourself in their place. Tsuzuki's work is a commentary on consumer culture and casts an empathetic eye on the mirror of aspiration that the clothing provides. A chance for the wearer to mentally escape from the four walls that contain them and their wardrobe. It's brand loyalty to the point of obsession. While I don't interpret the photographs themselves as judgemental or moralistic, it's notable that such habits were something the artist felt were well worth capturing, to be discussed and preserved for posterity.

Instead of thinking about which brands are best, it makes far more sense to analyse each potential purchase instead to determine whether it is a sustainable buy.

A sustainable buy looks at several factors:

1. Is it made well or to a standard appropriate to its price?
2. Is it something you still need/want after your wardrobe audit?
3. Does it contain synthetics when it's unnecessary (most everyday clothing does not require plastics to be used)?
4. Does the garment align with your lifestyle?
5. Is it sustainable for you financially?

There are brands out there that are doing a fantastic job in authentically speaking about their sustainability agenda, while providing an important point of view to the fashion industry. I hope that their stories will be inspiring to you. These founders, with their missions and brands are also great case studies in what the Mindful Monday Method looks for when evaluating whether a brand reliably produces sustainable buys. One such example may (or may not) come as a surprise to you.

Attire the Studio, a brand headed by super-influencer Xenia Adonts, began its journey ticking almost every box on the sustainable fashion brand checklist – from disclosing every factory and detailing their search for the lowest-impact fabrics to producing limited runs and only bringing back sell-throughs. And then the huge one that most brands have barely begun to crack – the brand successfully avoids producing micro-trends or using pressurising sales tactics that encourage impulsive consumption. In ways that huge brands could only dream of, Attire the Studio's e-commerce site claim of 'transparent, eco-friendly and ethical production – without compromising on quality or design' currently goes uncontested.

Take, for example, an everyday blazer, a staple that most professionals reach for. When I review one of these, I first look to see if there are any visual defects like asymmetry, snags, loose buttons or even misaligned patterns. Next, I check if the pockets are real, if the lining is cut properly to the size of the garment and whether the seams, particularly around the shoulder and armpit area, are loose. Then I move onto the composition tag. The materials listed don't have to include things like interlining, the fabric part of zips or what the thread is made of. You can safely assume that these are synthetic based – after all, nylon or polyester thread is heavy-duty and it makes sense to use something strong for these elements. So when I read the label and talk about the shell of a jacket being biodegradable, we aren't even touching on the other components that will only reveal themselves if we were to cut it open.

Even more substantial than a strip of reinforcement or scraps of string being synthetic are shoulder pads. These also don't need to be listed on the care labels. However, when Xenia Adonts promises fully biodegradable, she means it. The padding of her label's jackets are 100 per cent natural and it isn't an easy feat. 'There is always an easier path, especially when you don't even have to disclose certain information, but that's not how you create change in the industry. The extra mile is never crowded,' she tells me. Effort sets brands apart, particularly when one like this could rest on the laurels of its creator but chooses to set a new standard in fashion.

Digital creators are no strangers to flogging fashion to their audiences in the form of affiliate links, curated edits with fashion brands or even launching their own apparel businesses. Sustainable is the go-to theme for celebrity and influencer business ventures but very few are remotely convincing. They're often accompanied by taglines like 'pre-order', 'small factories' or 'made from deadstock materials', as if this alone is sufficient. Attire the Studio wants to be an example, a blueprint to others in the industry: 'Sustainability can be defined in many different ways and Attire has its very own. For us, transparency is the main value, everything else follows automatically.' Which is a noble way to hold a brand accountable. Xenia made Forbes 30 Under 30 in 2021, in the retail and e-commerce category, after her new-born brand reported growth of revenue to $1.2 million that year. It can pay handsomely to be different.

If the grass is greenwashed on the other side, on this part of the track, London-based With Nothing Underneath is a British B-Corp label founded by ex- Condé Nast editor, Philippa Durrell. We can call her Pip for short, she said so. It specialises in the one thing all genders have in their closet – the shirt. In fact, it's designed with buttons facing to the right, which is the 'menswear' way. Womenswear has buttons facing to the left, following the tradition that they were dressed by someone else.

I ventured into the brand's boutique in Sloane Square, its first physical space, armed with a ton of questions. Deep inside the shop, by the out-of-use fireplace, there are two accent chairs and curtain blinds in matching pinstripe cotton poplin. I was later told these are made of the same material as the shirts to avoid wasting the rest of that fabric roll.

It's not just surface-level stuff. With Nothing Under-neath is a fast-growing shirt brand that uses exclusively natural materials. That's right, not a polyester weave in sight. Fabrics like brushed cotton and merino wool (they assure me that the wool is non-mulesed), 100 per cent organic cotton for the seersucker and poplin styles, cosy cashmere and recycled silk. WNU has become somewhat of a cult brand for UK women and their boyfriends who are in the know. And I know £100 isn't cheap but it's well priced when you consider that the hands that made it were fairly paid, the fabrics are premium and even without experience you can tell that they're great quality simply by handling the garments. At the time of writing, all of its production takes place in Portugal, which the founders visit several times a year. There was about an hour of quizzing the marketing manager about the composition, right down to what the buttons are made of (corozo nut, river shell and mother of pearl – they sold through their recycled polyester button shirts and tell me that they have no intention of bringing back the plastic). The fact that someone who wasn't the owner or garment tech (sometimes founders don't even know the specifics) could answer 99 per cent of the questions was already impressive. Most brands simply look like they care; this one actually hires people that do.

From my experience, most brands that didn't start yesterday don't begin with a sustainability agenda. It's a relatively new demand that older brands are having to retrospectively apply, which costs them a lot of money, hence why many don't fully commit. Smaller, more nimble businesses tend to find it easier to adjust than larger ones. In both cases, it's ultimately how the brand has chosen to develop that's more important than whether or not it began with the purest of intentions.

Pip is honest about it. Her brand started with 'creating a basic shirt at a price point that wasn't ridiculous. It was about price point and quality'. In 2017, the options to buy new women's shirts were mainly an afterthought on the high street or something 'affordable' luxury brands were selling for £200 and more. I asked her how she plans to sustain the high standards that they currently hold as the brand grows, as so many before her have failed to do so in the name of profit. To that she answered, 'In the same way you want quality items to last forever, you want your reputation to last forever.'

Another source of inspiration for aspiring brands comes from one that I admire, E.L.V Denim (East London Vintage Denim). This is a great example of a 'zero waste' business that's scalable. Stylist turned fashion entrepreneur Anna Foster is a true recycling buff – her passion is utilising waste as the fantastic resource that it is. In 2022, she launched a collection with designer Gabriela Hearst. The capsule came about after spotting Hearst at the British Fashion Awards and approaching her with the idea. If you could only see the pieces in person, you'd understand that no one needs that much convincing to fall in love with them.

Foster sources secondhand deadstock from suppliers in the north of England, looking for jeans that second-hand retailers would pass up as too damaged or because its sizes that are too hard to sell. They are taken to their local cleaners in Hackney and then onto the E.L.V. studio. Here, the denim is assessed and graded as M for materials (for trousers that have too many flaws and need repurposing) or sorted according to size to be reworked into the signature four-seam trouser. This is an important factor as this unique construction allows the jeans to be tailored to size. In fact, it's what makes it possible for Anna and the team to create any size you wish, using the exact same concept of recycling jeans. The majority of their manufacturing has historically taken place at the highly prestigious Black Horse Lane Atelier. A name that has denim fanatics nodding their head in approval.

You can imagine, it's something of a laborious and intimate process. Everything is considered, from which shades of blue best complement one another to discussions over how many two-tone jeans should be created. I've seen first-hand how the small, all-female team manually arranges the patchwork of indigo rectangles to create a new textile. You can see the time, the love and the thought processes. You can feel it when you slide your legs into the crumply soft, thick denim without an ounce of elastane. What's fantastic about E.L.V. is that they've committed to repairing any of their products for free, for its lifetime. You might've thought that this is surely a positive marketing tool. The truth is, there is no financial gain to be made from this assurance (or luxury brands would be openly offering it too). It might soothe customers who aren't used to paying over £100 for a pair of jeans but this level of care comes from brands that have founders who genuinely care about the future of the fashion industry.

Is it worth it?

The following graphs are a visual representation of the quality versus the cost of popular brands across the fast fashion, premium and luxury price categories.

I've chosen to show them on an axis to demonstrate how similar these brands are to each other, in a bid to combat the perception that brands are vastly unique. We must remember that we, the individual, are the vehicle for our self-expression. These brands aim to sell a lifestyle or a dream which customers align themselves with, identifiable mainly by aesthetic. They can facilitate this, but they must do a lot more for us to deserve our loyalty. Simply giving us cute collections isn't enough. We cannot only think about style without the substance or we tumble into the marketing pitfalls that we are what we wear and that we should rely on brands.

You'll see through their performance according to the Mindful Monday Method that a lot of them are skewed towards being priced too high for the standard of construction. Sustainability has not been factored into these scores but the consistency of material choices have influenced them.

Fast Fashion

- ✦ These charts have been adjusted against the average price point and quality within its tier. For example, the fast fashion graph cannot be directly overlayed on the mid-tier or luxury one.
- ✦ These are based on in-store Mindful Monday Method reviews from 2019–23.
- ✦ These graphs do not consider sustainability initiatives or claims.

From the fast fashion graph, we can see that many of the brands overlap and that the difference between them, with regard to price and quality, is almost negligible. An interesting anecdote that I've heard from friends and even skimming through comments from video reviews is that some believe that one fast fashion brand is 'better' than another. Forgive the bluntness, but how this is substantiated is questionable.

When shopping with a modest budget, most of us know that it's impossible to expect couture quality for the price of a McDonald's meal. But the point is to learn how the fashion industry works to shop better quality. This is especially important to know if fast fashion stores will remain your go-to. So the industry operates on a volume basis. Let's say I had £30 to spare on an item. I wouldn't even waste my time looking at stores that churn out hundreds of stock keeping units, otherwise known as SKUs for short (a series of numbers that distinguish what the items are), of micro-trend led items. Brands that toe the line between fast fashion and slightly more premium also won't be friendly for this budget. The key thing is to look for natural fibres and a garment that has a simple pattern without needing to fit a particular way – as we learnt in Chapter One, fittings require time and models and will add to the overall cost.

The type of retailer to go for would be one with very few microtrends and lots of outfit 'basics'. When it comes to the brands on the graph, we would be hard-pressed to call any of them sustainable – capsule collections or not. But based on the price and quality axis, the clear outlier is Uniqlo.

This is an interesting brand because it's not your typical 'fashion' retailer. Although it also outsources to third party manufacturers, it owns some of its own factories which is quite rare. Less rare but notable is that it doesn't produce wholesale and thus its margins are large, meaning that more profit can be made. Uniqlo also focuses mainly on basics, performance wear such as thermals and cold weather coats, and it shies away from granular trends. They're relatively simple designs that don't cost a lot to make. Their production is high volume and therefore the company can use this to its advantage to price low.

The problem with the pricing of many of the brands highlighted here is that they sell things *seem* like they should cost more, so they have an inordinate price tag. Take knitwear, a category that shoppers tend to stomach paying more for because it's seasonal. It's seen as practical and it's associated with signifiers of quality, such as natural wool (although many of these items produced by fast fashion brands have a minority percentage of actual wool). Mass market knitwear (so this is something to watch out for across all brands) is heavily reliant on machine production, which is faster and cheaper. Therefore it doesn't require as much human labour as something like soft fabrics that are essentially human made. Hands are needed to work a sewing machine, aren't they? The takeaway here is that brands will get away with what they can but now you know how the fashion industry works, you can make the decision for yourself whether you'll accept it.

Quality

H&M Group

H&M (Hennes & Mauritz) was officially founded in 1947 and since then has grown to be one of the top apparel retailers, reporting $21.4 billion USD by the end of its fiscal year in 2022.[xxvi] Since 2006, it's been acquiring brands, starting with Monki and followed by COS in 2007, Weekday in 2008, & Other Stories in 2013 and Arket in 2017.

Having spoken to friends that work in the industry, it's understood that these brands operate relatively independently. Interestingly, COS and Arket are relatively similar in terms of quality of clothing and also have a similar price point. For example, suiting is a category that both names do to a high standard that are almost equal to each other. & Other Stories has an interesting design perspective, splitting their collections into 'ateliers' based on different fashion-forward cities with distinct styles like Stockholm, Paris or LA. Although you can definitely find your wardrobe basics here, it tends to lead to more trend-led garments, which you will have learnt by now means that it's as important as ever to check each item you're interested in thoroughly. This particular label uses a similar playbook to H&M, who are known for being a pioneer in luxe-meets-high-street collaborations. Designer collections include cult designers such as Rodarte, Rejina Pyo and A.W.A.K.E. Mode. It's interesting that the quality of these, with regard to the finishing, material choices and fit, doesn't increase drastically from its main lines.

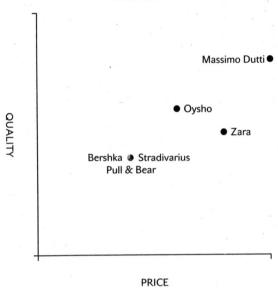

Inditex is a Spanish fashion conglomerate that was founded in 1985, by Amancio Ortega. It's best known for its flagship brand, Zara. Although it owns more than these brands in its portfolio, I've chosen to chart the most well-known and globalised names. At the bottom is a cluster of Bershka, Stradivarius and Pull & Bear. Not just aesthetically but in terms of price point and quality, these aren't significantly distinguishable from one another. On top of that, these three labels target a younger audience than the higher-quality names like Massimo Dutti or even Zara's mainline. I find it poses a much larger problem than just being an example of fast fashion. This is because it's generally acknowledged that younger people have less spending power than, say, those who have been in the workforce for several years. However, I feel that fast fashion has a dangerous way of reinforcing toxic shopping habits in youths. It positions itself as a 'good value deal' by offering low prices. But it also skimps hugely on the quality of construction, otherwise known as planned obsolescence. Let's put sustainability aside for a moment here.

If our clothes are going to fall apart well before we get our money's worth, doesn't that mean that we're more likely to find a replacement for them? If that doesn't sound like taking advantage of a group of people that can't afford to spend much on a single piece of apparel, I don't know what does. It's banking heavily on the fact that the customers won't care and even desire buying new and more frequently. Fast fashion brands like these are instrumental in training us to see shopping as a hobby.

The design of Zara's garments is slightly more complex than many of the other Inditex brands. It's built on its responsiveness to fashion trends and its stores are strategically placed in affluent areas, often in beautiful buildings. In the city of Zurich in Switzerland, it sits on the same road as Gucci and Hermès, albeit further down the street. In London there are many stores but a very large Zara sits directly opposite Harrods in Knightsbridge. In Paris, it's on the illustrious Champs-Élysées and in New York on prime fashion street, Fifth Avenue. The last two are perhaps a little less noticeable as other fashion giants dominate the sidewalks too, but one thing that's notable is that the others are unapologetically fast fashion. Zara presents itself as premium but shoppers lament that there's a lack of a reliable fit, that materials don't last – zips break quickly, buttons fall off within a wear or two and the clothes don't wash well.

Massimo Dutti serves as an interesting example as it's painfully obvious that it's much better made in terms of construction and material choice not just within the Inditex portfolio but compared to competitors. Clearly, there are the resources and infrastructure in place for decent-quality garments but this suggests to me that it's entirely intentional that the other brands serve up the equivalent of a chicken nugget while Massimo Dutti is the full Sunday roast. It is considerably more expensive, there's no denying that. But as much as it makes me unpopular amongst the sustainable fashion crowd, I'll call it as it is. Since reviewing brands in 2019 until present day, most of the items there are good quality for premium fashion. The real issue is whether or not they're sustainable buys.

Mid-Tier Brands

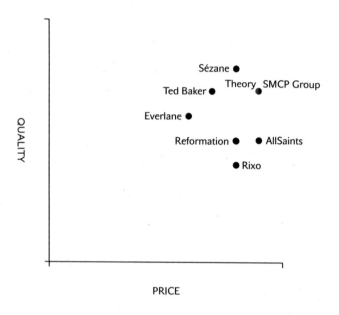

The temptation may be to look at a graph like this and pick out the SMCP group that owns Claudie Pierlot, Sandro and Maje to be some of the best mid-tier brands. I can't stress enough how that's not what the graphs demonstrate. The reason that we see the likes of Ted Baker and SCMP at first appear to be the better options is because of the complexity of their designs. The use of time-consuming trims, French seams or bias binding that's executed to a decent level is consistent and frequently spotted across their collections. Simply put, they put more effort into their garments across all of its categories in comparison to others on this graph.

The mid-tier level is also far more complex than fast fashion or luxury brands. The margins are tighter and several factors affect this. Firstly, a lot of them are brands that have popped up in the last decade. These don't have the reputation (of showing at Fashion Week and setting the trends or boasting an illustrious creative director, for example) or heritage to inflate their prices the way that the high-end labels do. Secondly, brands like this are constantly undermined by the lower-priced brands that offer the 'look for less', and if these premium brands don't use clout or quality to set themselves apart, they will lose out to better-value fashion.

Related to this point, the collections produced by the mid-tier category compared to the fast fashion retailers and high-end designer labels fluctuate in quality quite noticeably. It often means that from season to season, the number of items that pass the Mindful Monday Method rise and fall more than the other price categories. In this sense, they're some of the least reliable places to shop, yet they're perceived as comfortably aspirational options – a palatable halfway point between fast fashion and luxury fashion. This isn't to suggest that they're not worth considering – far from it. I have personally bought products from these names or recommended garments from there before – but not without using the Mindful Monday Method first. It's this premium category where we need to practise even more discernment.

Luxury Brands

When I started charting these brands, I was hyperaware of how contentious it can be – especially when discussing luxury brands that seem to command such loyalty that they are like a cult of personality. Again, it's important to note that quality can differ and this might change under new creative leadership or a different CEO.

Emerging or cult designers such as Jacquemus, Toteme and Zimmermann have been included in the luxury brand list. I asked my audience what they thought of this and the majority firmly stated that these labels are not in the same league as super brands like Chanel,

Christian Dior and Prada. I chose to include the more accessible emerging brands anyway because they vie for the same customer. There are plenty of shoppers who may be basing their purchase decisions on what's popular as opposed to what's worth the investment. They'll be considering these brands almost as equals, where they believe cultural value to be more significant than material value.

More than that, when it comes to those already planning to shop at a luxury brand, cost acts as an accelerator if it's considered 'affordable' in the designer sphere. For example, in the case of a Toteme coat for under £800 or a mini bag from Jacquemus for under £1,000. Or it may act as a brake, in the case of parting with nearly £900 for a pair of jeans, which is a price tag consistently seen at the ultra high-end maisons on the graph.

A couple of these names stood out to me while I was collating their average prices across garment categories. Bottega Veneta, as an example, holds an extremely high price tag in my mind because I associate this brand as having one of the best quality leather goods. However, when I was squaring up the cost of its clothing (leather accessories have not been factored into this graph) in comparison to the other luxury brands, I noticed that on average, buying a garment here is more or less the same. The interesting thing about luxury fashion is that most of what we see is from editorials or items pulled by stylists for celebrities. Usually, these are the statement-making pieces that command a heftier price.

In actuality, the majority of garments produced by designers (at least the ones featured on this graph) are wearable every day.

Generally speaking, when buying from a luxury brand, there's an element of getting what you pay for – at least within the context of each other. The outliers of what is subpar to the main players are quite clear. What we do know as shoppers is that value is more important than purchasing the theoretical 'absolute best' available. For the sake of argument, take a tank top using the finest fibres that retails for £1,000. In reality, while this may be top-tier quality, most individuals would do much better with a top using a good weight (meaning that it's smooth in texture and not see-through) of cotton instead. It's easier to launder and maintain, and if you can buy the right one, it's the same 'value'. This is precisely what we're looking for when we talk about an item being 'worth it'. Just because you can afford the most expensive, doesn't mean it's wise to pay for it.

Made in our imagination

'Hey Andrea, would it be possible to talk about luxury brands that are made in China and the quality?' one viewer asked and I was more than happy to answer.

There is the illusion that where a garment was made matters these days. Once upon a time, in 1887, it did. Surprisingly, even though when we think of appellations we think of the French, this law actually originated in Britain. It was a way to differentiate British goods from German-made products at a turning point of the industrialisation of Europe. It's interesting to see a history of Britishness repeatedly referenced in heritage brands and exaggeratedly so in menswear. Names such as Dunhill and Private White VC have bragging rights as they are some of the remaining minority to produce in the UK. However, the majority of brands – even some of the names that sell on Savile Row – don't. As we've touched on before, it's a form of generating cultural value through association of a prestigious Made In label. Storytelling and history doesn't have a price tag per se, but we know that if it did, it would have a lot of zeros.

The idea of buying from the country you're in has a patriotic element. 'Buy British' is a recurring theme we see whenever the UK is in turmoil; for example, the first time it appears is in the late 1800s to counteract the threat from German production. Later, during the Great Depression, it was employed to support domestic industries to boost the economy. In 1968, 'I'm Backing Britain' was another campaign with the same goal as the state coffers were in a great deficit. Though now, globalisation means that even if we wanted to exclusively support British businesses, it's a lot harder to do so with entangled supply chains.

For example, Burberry is arguably seen as the backbone of the British fashion industry. It can present runway shows outside of the London Fashion Week schedule and it'll still command an A-list turnout, supermodels to walk and press that any other designer could only dream of. The brand claims to manufacture 'at Burberry-owned sites in the UK and Italy, as well as through a network of global suppliers'. The 'network' could really mean anywhere. Then there's Barbour, a brand that brings to mind waxed jackets, Agas and damp spaniels. Or if you're a royalist, Queen Elizabeth II traipsing around the Scottish Highlands with her corgis. The countryside outfitters is known for its site in South Shields in the UK, but as it's a global brand, it's difficult to imagine that a facility like this could accommodate its volumes. Let's not forget Doc Martens. The beloved bootmaker of the rock and roll and fashion crowd has a specific 'Made In England' range. A *Guardian* article reported that just 2 per cent of their styles are still manufactured in the UK and that the shift to China began as early as 2004.[xxvii]

It's worth noting that producing in China has become the expensive option. Things have changed but biased perceptions haven't quite caught up. There was a time in the not so distant past when production in Indonesia stopped being economical. Once, I found myself at dinner with the owner of a knitwear factory, who told me that she lost a lot of business when employee welfare laws kicked in, in 2018. This meant that labour costs went up and huge retailers, ones you probably have in your wardrobe right now, refused to pay for it. It's not that the factory owners didn't want to accommodate the regulation, it's more that huge brands simply didn't feel the need to fork out extra. So these fashion businesses moved on to another country where wages are less regulated and manufacturing would stay cheap. They go to places like Bangladesh, which, according to the World Trade Organization (WTO), surpassed China as the world's largest exporter of apparel in 2010.

Going back to the question posed by a viewer, the 'Made In' labelling is very much a myth. Globalisation and the easy flow of goods around the world is cited as the cause for laxity around the disclosure of where a product is actually made. If that's even possible to find out. Honestly, it may not even be a case of brands not wanting to tell us, although I'm sure greenhushing is a part of the reason why. In actuality, most brands cannot tell you all the countries that a particular garment has passed through because they genuinely do not know, it's costly and they don't see any financial gain in discovering this. Don't open Pandora's box, basically.

Fashion Revolution's 2022 Transparency Index did not report any brands exceeding 81 per cent. A score of this and above would mean that the brand discloses 95 per cent of its suppliers across its pipeline, its policies on purchasing practices and how it intends to go about paying workers a living wage. The brands would also reveal its water usage, carbon footprint and use of renewable energy from its own operations. If you're interested to know, the lowest-scoring category contains luxury brands and fast fashion alike. A stark finding was that 96 per cent of brands don't disclose the number of workers in its supply chain who are paid a living wage. Bear in mind that the living wage in many countries where factories are situated is significantly lower than what we in the global north would imagine. It really begs the question, how bad is it that you need to hide it? Fashion Nova, Revolve and Dolce & Gabbana sit side by side here.

Sustainable fashion is at the precipice of change. Legislation like The Fashion Act demands brands that sell in the state of New York to bi-annually report on a large number of data points. For example, information about suppliers like who they are, where they're based, the percentage of unionised factories, as well as the frequency of workers' overtime, just to name a few. It's a bill that involves due diligence and will be enforced by the Attorney General. It's also validated by an independent third party, which is a large differentiator from the sustainability measuring tools we looked at earlier. One of its goals is to improve human rights. It's essential to think about the quality of life for garment workers when we think about the quality of our clothing.

'Made In' is really something that we romanticise in our imaginations, not a quality assurance, confidence that your items haven't been made in a sweatshop or a statement of patriotism. In theory, a shirt can be partially manufactured in Bangladesh, shipped to England and labelled as 'Made in the UK', as long as it was assembled or an element of it was finished in that country. Truly, very few things can go from soil to retail stores and stay within the same territory. An endeavour like this would look like slow fashion, involving localised supply chains and perhaps even an element of localised design too.

As for other countries, the US has stricter rules. The Federal Trade Commission states that, '"Made in USA" means that "all or virtually all" the product has been made in America. That is, all significant parts, processing and labour that go into the product must be of US origin'.[xxviii]

On one of my field trips, I visited a design studio in east London (where else?). It's situated by a canal and a multitude of British designers like Simone Rocha and Self-Portrait reside nearby. Here, I was shown what a fully factored operation looks like, one where everything from white label designs to completed garments are created. I walked into a sunny open space, kitted out with a dining table enclosed by a library of fabric swatches and partial samples of clothing. The racks of half-pieces, signifying the fronts or backs of garments, showcase what is possible for the factory to manufacture, based on forecasted trends. The factory is situated in China and run by a French family, with an office in the UK. When I put it like that, it sounds incredibly international but at the time, I didn't blink twice. Supply chains like these are the norm.

I was shown a dress by a brand I recognise – I had been gifted a gorgeous silk maxi dress by their PR agency before. I was familiar with its great quality. Even though its aesthetic no longer appeals to me, it's a piece I find hard to part with and I'd have a hard time considering selling it on because it's just so well crafted. I was told that the intricate screen printing, hot fix crystal applications and lace appliqué that's part of the brand's visual DNA can take up to two weeks to create. With a price point hovering around the high three figures, it's easy to see why. And it's unashamedly made in China. The studio showed me a slick catalogue of the other brands that it sews for, like Ted Baker, Me+Em and Paul Smith to name a few. All of which are British. They were careful to tell me that they are not the only factory that makes the clothes for these companies, just one of many.

According to Asia Garment Hub, an online information resource hub, clothing manufacturing in China is currently worth $150 billion USD and accounts for 7.1 per cent of its GDP. The benefit to manufacturing in a country that invests so heavily at all stages of the supply chain is that this is also where the most innovation happens. Some common examples that you might find in your wardrobe are digital printing for textiles like graphic t-shirts and seamless knitting, which you can easily find examples of in sportswear (the conventional method would be cut and sew, linking panels of knitting together). The design studio I visited was thrilled to share with me that their Chinese factory uses AVITERA® SE, an 'eco-friendly' dye created by Huntsman Corporation. The innovation claims to reduce water usage by 50 per cent, using 15–20 litres of water for one kilogram of material, compared to what could be up to 100 litres for hot dyeing systems. This new dye requires fewer rinsing baths (which are used to rinse off excess colour).

'Made in China' follows the laws of supply and demand: where there is most demand the likelihood of progress, improved technology and even sustainable innovations are higher.

It's really the luxury retailers that need to own up to the false notion that skilled labour can be determined by which hemisphere it's in. It serves as a distraction from the industrialised scale at which expensive goods are produced and attempt to disassociate them from lower-end retailers. Many labels that position themselves as premium or luxury produce their garments in the same factories, using the same labour conditions as their mass-fashion counterparts.

Jewellery

In this section, we'll be learning about what the differences are among plating, vermeil and filled jewellery. We'll take a look at what's appropriate for your intended use and frequency of wear. I'll also share with you some of the ethical certifications that you can look for and by the end, you'll be more assured on how to shop for quality jewellery.

We'll be focusing on semi-fine and fine jewellery, because of its proximity to fashion.

Above this, in the high jewellery category we're looking at the likes of Boucheron and Repossi. If you're lucky enough to be shopping there, I don't think you'll need to worry so much about quality!

When we talk about semi-fine jewellery, we're referring to accessories that contain gemstones and/or precious metals. There's a contentious debate over whether semi-fine jewellery is ever 'worth it', given its low precious metal content.

I have two semi-fine pieces that I wear all the time that haven't failed me over years of wear – I don't take them off, even in the shower, the ocean, swimming pools, the gym and I even sleep with them on. One item is a gold cross pendant from a British brand and another is a vintage-style necklace from a French-owned costume jewellery business. Both are 18-carat gold-plated and have never tarnished but when they do, my plan is to invest in restoring rather than replacing them. Just like clothing, metals can wear down and need maintenance. So it's entirely normal to have to replate your jewellery to maintain its lustrous gold coating.

AMOUNT OF CARAT GOLD	PURITY	USE
9k	37.5 per cent gold	Extremely hard as it's mainly alloys.
14k	58.5 per cent	Hard and durable but very little gold – almost half is made up of metal alloys.
18k	75 per cent	Suitable for everyday wear and containing a substantial amount of precious metal.
22k	91.6 per cent	Used for fine jewellery as it's a high percentage of gold with other metals for durability.
24k	99.9 per cent	Purest form of gold, extremely soft and often purchased as an investment.

Why recycled metals aren't 'sustainable'

Metals come from three main sources: recycling, for example from an existing piece of jewellery; recycled metals from a refinery or directly from a mine. There are niche sources that are arising because of the demand for a more 'sustainable' source, such as e-waste, where precious metals like gold can be obtained in tiny quantities from household items – things like your phone, laptop or even speakers. Although definitely not enough to warrant the rising iPhone prices, but I digress. There are alternative ways for jewellery brands to buy metals from its source – for example, working with a cooperative to purchase panned gold. I'm told of a female cooperative in Choco, Colombia, that does this as and when they need the cash. Aware of their finite resources, they only take from nature what they need and want to protect it as a financial resource for their children. As you may have deduced, this is only available to purchase on a small scale as supply isn't steady.

The key thing to note if you're sustainably inclined is that when you're considering a new piece of jewellery, aim for the brand to tick a few more boxes than using recycled metals. As always, we bring it back to quality. Some things can be really hard to tell if you're not an expert but there are plenty of common sense points that can help you spot a potentially high-risk purchase. There are design elements that could lead to a piece causing issues later on. Let's use a ring with a gemstone in it as an example. Firstly, find out its caratage, otherwise known as its purity, because anything at 24 carats is extremely malleable and isn't a wise decision for everyday, wearable jewellery – it's far too soft. Instead, opt for something around 18-carat gold because it's hard enough to be worn often but has a sweet spot in gold-to-alloy content. Secondly, take note of the claws that are holding the gem, do they look sturdy enough for the size of the stone? There may be a temptation to go for a setting where there are hardly any prongs for a trendy 'minimalist' look but this could be disastrous. No one wants a Kim K in the ocean moment when they discover that their diamond is missing.

Thirdly, how thick is the ring itself? I've seen the most beautiful 'floating' rings where gems are threaded through clear elastic so that the band is seemingly invisible. Or designs where stones set on delicate links, but this will be extremely prone to breakage as we can be quite rough with our hands and chains are fragile. The band of a ring is called a shank and experts say that it should be no less than 2mm, which is generally the thinnest across the industry standard because ultra-skinny shanks will wear down and weaken over time.

Vermeil, filled, plated and gold tone

The structural integrity of jewellery is important, as is the precious metal content. However, there are varying degrees of thickness and not all are equal.

TYPE	WHAT IT'S MADE OF	VALUE	HOW TO CARE FOR IT
Gold tone	Copper and zinc to create the hue of yellow gold.	This is costume jewellery and can easily tarnish.	Do not let it get wet. Over time, oxidation will occur and can stain your skin green.
Gold plated	Gold thickness over a metal alloy, greater than or equal to 0.5 microns. Alloys are commonly copper or brass.	Close to costume jewellery, this is a little more hard-wearing. This kind of jewellery is unlikely to have or retain monetary value.	Replate every one to two years, depending on frequency of use and the purity of gold.

TYPE	WHAT IT'S MADE OF	VALUE	HOW TO CARE FOR IT
Vermeil	Gold thickness over sterling silver greater than or equal to 2.5 microns.	This is a thicker gold plating over another precious metal. It's a more valuable piece and many examples are priced as accessible luxury.	Replate every one to two years, depending on frequency of use and the purity of gold.
Gold-filled	Gold weight is 5 per cent over brass or sterling silver.	Higher-quality materials are used and the gold is a much thicker coating.	Replate every one to two years, depending on frequency of use and the purity of gold.
Solid gold	Gold without a base metal, where its purity is defined by carat.	This is the most valuable and potentially heading towards fine jewellery, depending on the piece and the purity of gold used.	Depending on the purity of gold, which is a direct correlation to its softness, the thickness of the piece should be considered as it can eventually wear away. Polishing may be required.

What should I buy?

Finding out that jewellery is yet another one of the categories – such as lingerie and sportswear – that is inherently difficult to be considered 'sustainable', can be off-putting to some. I see the temptation in throwing all caution to the wind and just buying whatever you feel like – after all, you'll wear it all the time anyway. There are other routes that you can take beyond simply prioritising quality, which is what we just learnt about. If your shopping goal is to buy less, buy better or shop from an independent brand then it's worth considering further nuances. For example, the rise of lab-grown diamonds (and other gems) has made a grab at the sustainability claim. These are man-made using a diamond 'seed', a rather sweet name for a tiny starter stone. Its quality and size will influence the final product. This is built up to form a larger gem using either of two methods: chemical vapour deposition (CVD) or high pressure-high temperature (HPHT), which mimic conditions of the earth's mantle. It takes weeks to months – as opposed to the millions of years that it would take to create a small diamond – and the process is highly energy-intensive. This innovation has been around for longer than its boom – around 2021 – when fashion jewellery giant Pandora first debuted a collection using synthetic diamonds. They're certainly not the first pioneers of lab grown gems but as we discussed in Supply and Demand, the largest brands pave the way for others in the industry, in terms of educating customers and creating desirability.

However, critics of lab-grown stones might argue that the amount of energy it takes to create a diamond is wholly unsustainable. Although, compared to the devastating environmental impact of opening a mine, 250–750 kWh to create a one-carat stone doesn't seem as intense. Another argument is that there are plenty of gems in circulation that can be repurposed, so not every rock needs to be bought 'new' from a mine. Just like how metals can be melted down and recycled.

When it comes to the iconic diamond, this is highly controlled, and some may claim it to be a monopolised gemstone. Worldwide, reserves have been depleting. Some recent closures such as the Williamson Mine in Tanzania (2020), Victor Mine in Canada (2019) and Premier Mine or Cullinan Mine (2008) are high-profile examples of just how unsustainable it is to continue taking from the earth. There may be more mines discovered in the future but ultimately, this serves as a reminder that what cannot be regenerated surely cannot be 'sustainable'.

The price of diamonds is also fairly arbitrary, making them a beautiful thing to own but also inflated by status. If we are to think of it in terms of cultural and material value, this would sway slightly towards hype. That's not to say diamonds aren't worth the investment or that they're unworthy of the high praise, they just aren't for everyone. It all began in 1888, when De Beers took control of several diamond mines in South Africa by consolidating them and buying exclusive mining rights. The goal was to control output through stockpiling gems and by creating the Central Selling Organisation (CSO) in 1934. The cartel aggregated uncut stones and distributed them to approved traders and manufacturers, also known as 'sightholders'. In controlling who could buy the vast majority of diamonds available and how many they could have, De Beers controlled the market price. While its grip has waned over time, the company still has profound influence. After all, it was their marketing campaign that implanted the idea of a diamond engagement ring and nothing else into the minds of those about to propose, all over the world.

An example of a jeweller that's doing it right is Pippa Small. I first came across the London-based designer (originally an anthropologist) at a round-table discussion at a fashion school in Mayfair. She piqued my interest when she proclaimed to us, 'There is no such thing as sustainable jewellery.' A moment of applause, please. A few months later, I visited her hot pink boutique in Notting Hill.

Pippa's business model is incredibly unique, much like many of the brands I've chosen to highlight in this book. All have proved that going against the grain and surviving in the fashion industry is possible. Challenging, but possible. The jeweller bases its sites of production in locations where people most need work. Places like Afghanistan, Myanmar, Colombia and Bolivia because, Pippa says, 'Anywhere where there's a lot of trouble, a job – any job – is the most precious thing because every person employed is kind of supporting 40 other people.'

An interesting example she provides is the work in Kibera, a large informal settlement that sits on the outskirts of Nairobi and is home to a population of over 100,000. The livelihoods of many here depend on recycling the enormous amounts of waste dumped at the Dandora landfill. This is reportedly the largest in

East Africa. According to the Textile Value Chain's 2019 report, it houses some of the 150 to 200 tonnes of textiles that the region receives every day, in addition to general waste. This is one of the places where Pippa Small pieces are crafted.

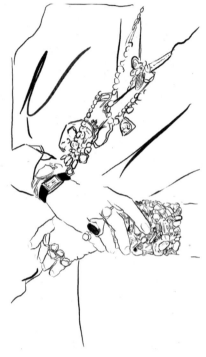

'We started working on recycled base metals to create jewellery. But one of the things was making chains, which is quite labour intensive, by hand. Each link is cut, soldered and polished. And we were able to make metres of it and think of as many designs using chains as possible . . . So it's something that doesn't take an enormous amount of skill but you need time and a certain amount of knowledge. They were able to pass that training on even to people they felt were worse off than them, in order to give them jobs.' She admits that it's an industry-wide problem that it's not always possible to tell where the materials used comes from but prioritising up-and-coming jewellers and independent businesses, asking questions about the origins of stones and feeling out whether or not you're comfortable with the answers is the most important.

It's also good to opt for stones outside of the big four: sapphire, diamond, ruby and emerald, which often have a hefty price tag because of the prestige attached to them. Although, it's worth knowing that there are lab-grown versions of these precious stones too. Buying from retailers with accreditations will give you more confidence that it's slightly more ethical. For example, the Responsible Jewellery Council conducts audits across the pipeline, from mines to the retailers, certifying ethical practice. It covers precious stones and metals like gold and platinum.

You may have heard the name Intertek pop up here before – this is a company that monitors the standards at manufacturing facilities. We've seen it in the context of testing fabric rolls for colour transfer, light degradation and friction (pilling). Intertek auditors assess sites for compliance with the Responsible Jewellery Council's standards. The RJC is made up of over 100 jewellery companies, such as the Diamond Trading Company (part of De Beers group) and Cartier. Critics say that it's not as 'independent' as you might want from an accreditation body and that there are more ethical ones available, like a Fair Trade assurance. At this stage of the sustainability journey, particularly with jewellery, this is one of the better options that we as customers have available. It's something we should consider, but with a pinch of salt.

Fairmined Gold and Fairmined Ecological Gold is an assurance that the gold comes from artisanal or other-wise known as 'small-scale' mines. These terms refer to operations that typically would use less machinery and chemicals. The accreditation guarantees the miners a minimum price and a premium. The difference between the two is that the latter promises no use of toxic chemicals (as opposed to 'responsible' use) and to restore ecosystems. It also carries a considerably more expensive surcharge. Fairtrade Certified Gold is another option to look into. This means that the metal is only sourced from small-scale mines that are protecting the environment and giving back to their communities. The website fairtrade.org.uk has a list of jewellery brands that use this more ethical alternative. If we're to look solely at material value, pawnshops are a potential source of fairer priced jewellery. However, I know that in some cultures, the response to wearing something as sentimental as someone's (intact) jewellery is that it could hold 'negative energy'.

If even the social justice missions that Pippa Small undertakes don't warrant being branded as 'sustainable' in her eyes, it tells you a lot about how murky and convoluted the industry is. And you thought fashion was complicated. Still, to purchase and own a piece, whether to commemorate an occasion or to add to your daily rotation of adornments, is a special moment. Jewellery is considered to have far more emotional value imbued in it than any other accessory. We don't have to purchase the most expensive pieces to invest in quality and there are great options at any price point. We just don't need to kid ourselves that jewellery brands are wholly sustainable.

Shoes

How are shoes made?

✴ A designer creates a design that is then used to
create a pattern, which breaks the shoe down into
its component pieces – similar to how garments
have multiple panels.

✴ Skiving is where the material for the shoe – for
example, leather, is thinned and trimmed.

✴ The shoe is stitched together and placed on
a 'last' – a mould shaped like a foot – to keep
the shoe in shape. This step is one of the most
important as it affects durability, comfort and
fit. However, brands that are trying to reduce
costs will use a generic last that hasn't been
fully customised to the type of shoe that's
manufactured. Have you ever tried on a shoe and
it doesn't touch every part of your foot, yet the
size seems to be correct? It may be that you have
trouble finding shoes that fit your feet in general
but it could also possibly show that the last used
was a poorer-quality one.

✴ How the sole is attached to the sock (the part of
the shoe that touches the foot) is one of the most
obvious indicators of a poor-quality shoe. When
it comes to planned obsolescence, soles can split
apart, be extremely heavy and unpleasant to
walk in, which encourages faster purchase of a
replacement pair. Soles can also be thin and wear

down easily, or improperly glued on so they come apart easily.

+ Finally, the shoe is polished and checked over before it's packed ready to ship.

What I have loved about the process of writing this book is meeting the people behind brands and hearing about their sometimes unlikely starts in the industry. I met Aneliya Kyurkchieva over Zoom during the pandemic when she launched the shoe brand House of Atana. She had left her job as an embroidery designer at Alexander McQueen and venturing into the world of footwear was entirely new to her. Starting from scratch, she was living in Bulgaria, sourcing suppliers and factories in Italy, learning how to run her own business and create a lookbook for her first collection. She told me that there are fittings for shoes using models that have sample size (a UK 4) and perfectly proportioned feet. The process sounds similar to how you might have a fit model for clothes. You can tell that with mass-market shoes, this is the part that is skipped in favour of cost saving. If you've ever struggled with shopping for shoes at fast-fashion brands, it's likely because you don't have Barbie-like feet. The shock!

When Aneliya began House of Atana, it wasn't about sustainability but highlighting quality. 'Shoes are not the most sustainable thing to make so let's be honest about that. You can still be responsible in decisions that you make and I think that makes a difference,' she said. And part of that responsibility lies in whether a shoe is made for virality or longevity. The embroidery designer turned footwear entrepreneur's words about focusing first on quality and a short supply chain instead of overly ambitious, confusing claims in the deep end of sustainability echoes the sentiment of Patricia Blaj, the founder of Loud Bodies. It also follows the thread of thought of Pip Durrell, the owner of With Nothing Underneath from earlier in Chapter Three. Perhaps we've found something here – simplify what 'sustainable fashion' actually means by humanising it and prioritising the people involved. That is, the individuals buying the product and the ones making it.

'They don't make them like they did when my mum bought them' and 'since selling out to private equity, the standards have slipped' are things I've heard from my friends and the Mindful Monday community.

'It' items or 'cult buys' aren't exactly the root of the problem. We know this because accessories with this coveted status have been around for a long time. Kids growing up in the late 1990s and early 2000s saw the Fendi Spy, Louis Vuitton's limited edition Speedy (the Takashi Murakami versions!).

The most interesting difference between now and two decades ago is the discourse about quality and wearability. These are factors that weren't so much of a hot take back when we'd see pap shots of Sienna Miller and Kate Moss clutching oversized bags in the crook of their arms. 'It' items have gotten to the point of near ludicrousness.

We are witnessing designs that look like only a doll could wear them – PVC Cinderella slippers, satin ballerina shoes with a slither of a sole, heels that have no ankle support and can't be walked in. And they are taking social media feeds by storm, without a word of how unpleasant they are to wear. This is beyond the infamous quote attributed to Christian Louboutin, 'High heels are pleasure with pain. If you can't walk in them, don't wear them.' There is nothing sexy or empowering about blood blisters and being poorer for it. Aneliya echoes this sentiment: 'Do you want to make shoes for Instagram?' she asks rhetorically.

Tips on how to shop for shoes:

- ✴ No visible glue on new shoes (image 1, page 270).
- ✴ The shoe should be stable when standing upright, not easily tipped over.
- ✴ The heel should feel sturdy and properly attached.
- ✴ Weight matters. It can be influenced by the design – for example, platform heels can be heavy and are difficult to walk in, be wary that constant use can potentially cause future health issues.
- ✴ The parts of the shoe touching the skin, like the straps, should be soft and supple.
- ✴ Leather shoes that have creases, slight wrinkles, etc. are a natural attribute of the material and suggest that the hide isn't heavily treated. This is

a good thing but it requires more maintenance and care from the wearer.

✴ Look for cushioned soles. A lot of brands that want to cut corners start by not opting for this step in the manufacturing process.

1   An example of visible glue on a designer shoe.

2   Here, the soft leather insole hasn't been cut to the correct size
    and the straps are lifting it off. Over time, this may detach as
    dirt and dust gets under and loosens the glue.

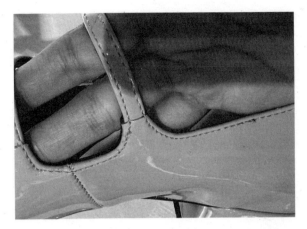

3 Poor execution of a Mary Jane style shoe from a fast fashion
brand. Here, you can see the haphazard joining of the strap to
the main part of the shoe.

4 This is an example of natural wear and tear. Over time and
especially with heat (from the environment or friction from
our feet) glue can loosen and appear. This needs cleaning
and maintenance.

5 Natural, soft leather will form creases over time, as seen in this example.

6 Another example of an insole badly fitted to the shoe. Here, instead of trimming it back, you can see wonky stitching as the manufacturers have tried to make it fit.

Summary

✦ Sustainable buys are the preferable way to
shop over looking for brands that claim to be
sustainable. This means learning your wardrobe
needs, budget and shopping goals in order to
look at individual items specifically rather than
buying solely from 'sustainable brands'.

✦ Quality is integral to eventually spending less on
fashion by buying less.

✦ Ethical accreditations can be useful but are not
the only measurement of a sustainable buy.

✦ 'Made in' labelling is mostly a marketing tool.
Thanks to globalisation and complex supply
chains, we cannot use the country on the label
as a mark of quality.

✦ Do not rely on a brand to create the same level
of quality across all of its product categories.
Budgets, design teams and even factories differ
here so the likelihood that it's inconsistent is
very high.

Chapter 6

BEYOND
FASHION

A t the heart of it, humans long to connect. We are simply looking for someone, something, some place, where we can feel safe. When it comes to fashion, there aren't too many of those around. The Mindful Monday Method was born from a place of trauma and brokenness, in my personal and professional life. I know people use that word 'trauma' a lot but I can assure you, I don't choose it flippantly. Because of this, I know that it takes a lot of hard work and will to change habits but I believe it's entirely possible because I made it through to the other side. It took around two years for me to really hone what I really wanted the method to achieve. If there's one wish I have for you at the end of this book, it's that you're able to break the habit of impulse shopping.

The Mindful Monday Method has helped me too and not just in giving me a chance to work in an industry that I love but felt excluded from. In 2022, at the age of 30, I got a diagnosis for ADHD. I always felt like I was doing life on level 10 difficulty and just couldn't understand why. Was I extremely sensitive? Was I genetically prone to anxiety and there was literally nothing I could do about it? Was I the problem?

The real answer was that I didn't have enough dopamine in my brain and struggled with executive functions and impulse control, among other things. That provided a lot of relief and validation, but it also made me realise how special the Mindful Monday Method actually is. I'm extremely cautious of remotely suggesting that this has any sort of scientific or medical backing whatsoever, so I will put it bluntly: it doesn't.

But what it did do for me was create a framework so that I could manage the symptoms of my ADHD, specifically the dopamine cravings and impulse shopping. The wardrobe audit helped me to rediscover items that I had forgotten about simply because I didn't see them. And doing this seasonally was life-changing. After two rounds of it, I really started to see the impact. Oh, and who could forget the laissez-faire attitude to money? The financial wellness exercises that I created for us targeted that vicious tennis match of overspending counteracted by bouts of austerity. In the past, I managed it OK because my tolerance for discomfort is pretty low. But my mental wellness kept taking the hit when I didn't feel fiscally stable. Not only did I feel I had nothing to wear but I also didn't really know what to do about it. Learning more about materials and honing my ability to recognise quality cemented my goal to shop more mindfully with circularity in mind.

My greatest hope is that this method supersedes me and my platforms. That it becomes a way of shopping that is larger than us all. I am far from the 'most sustainable' person that I know, whatever that means. But this is one of my contributions to a cause that I truly feel for.

And this is because if you look at the much, much larger picture than what's in our wardrobes, there are no plans to shrink gross domestic product (GDP) intentionally anywhere. Therefore, governments will not condone the degrowth of industries when their economies rely on it. Bangladesh is one of the greatest manufacturing hubs of fashion in the world. At the time of writing, it employs around 4 million people and its contribution to GDP is 11%, making garments its biggest export item. As for brands, corporate revenue targets only increase year on year and with that, volumes will increase and competition to put out the most appealing products continues – whether that's based on low cost, value, heritage or any of the other factors that brands tie to their commercial strategy. Attending conferences like the Global Fashion Agenda's Global Fashion Summit in Copenhagen highlighted to me how policymakers are striving to reach their [insert not so distant year here] goals. It has also revealed to me just how much brands are made up of innovative people who are just rearing to make changes happen where they are. To borrow a phrase my agent voicenoted me, they are 'chipping away at the marble until it becomes Michelangelo's David'. But I do think that how much we care about the future of the planet and how vocal we are will have an enormous influence on this. And why wait on the sidelines when there's so much we can do to improve our lives and those of others, now?

When we're battling against a machine so much larger than us, we need to ask ourselves, what are we doing it for? Let me propose something that might make me even less popular with the sustainability activists. What if we see the statistics, the contradicting studies and the overwhelming sense of the world ending, the sky falling and the polar bears disappearing (hopefully not) as important reference points, but not the narrative? What if it's about focusing on resolving our reliance on letting the clothes we wear define us? What if we honed in on the aspects of 'sustainability' that most spark our compassion?

You know that saying, learn to walk before you can run? I'd add that as you learn to walk, you're actually solving some of the foundational aspects of those larger problems. The Mindful Monday Method is designed not to be inspirational but actionable and educational. It produces results that could mean that we're all shoppers one day and changemakers the next. And for the superheroes out there not content with simply checking care labels – please know that this is no small feat. It's not menial. It's pretty fucking revolutionary to learn how to shop.

I know I say not to rely on brands and throughout this book, I have highlighted ones that have stood out to me. I have wondered if it matters whether or not many of these vulnerable, disruptive and young companies will still exist in a decade until I realised, it doesn't matter. They still existed, they still paved a way for alternative paths that didn't exist before in mainstream fashion. This is about being on the side of those who are forging alternative paths in a very challenging fashion industry. What's more, it's about proving that businesses, entrepreneurs and individuals can be successful in doing things the unconventional way.

Are you still confused? OK, shop like it's your wedding dress

I had an interesting thought one morning. Actually, it was two days away from this book's submission deadline. When I feel the fear that's when the best thoughts come to me. As I was drying my hair, I thought about the approach that we have to shopping when we know that the item we're going to buy has significance. And I pondered the one look that many of us are willing to put a certain level of investment and effort into. It's what you wear on your wedding day. What this means is different for everyone, but I think that we can universally accept that this is an occasion that a lot of people will consider carefully.

Maybe it's because I'm at the age when most of my friends are coupling up and driving off into the sunset in vintage gowns (it seems to be a trend at the moment and I'm into it) but it sparked the idea that perhaps everything we buy, everyday and occasionwear alike, should follow the approach that we take for 'The One' dress/suit/onesie – whatever makes your heart beat faster; we'll just refer to it as a dress for ease. It's like looking for your life partner, which I believe is someone that you consciously choose, rather than a soul that was made for you by the divine universe. Even bespoke dresses are decided on by you: the fabric, the length, the colour and the silhouette – I can't imagine many people letting a designer go hell for leather on a dress that they'll have zero say on.

Reflecting on the women around me, I see they've taken drastically different avenues to finding their outfit. One of my closest friends flew out to Italy for a dress fitting the day after she was proposed to. This masterpiece took two years to create. My cousin found her dress on Vinted two weeks after she got engaged and eight months out from her summer wedding, enough time to get it tailored. Charlotte Jacklin, who we met earlier in the book, told me her dress was custom-made as she knew she wouldn't find anything off the rack and it took four to five months. I asked my audience how long they took to find their wedding outfit and the answer varied wildly from 'the first one I tried on' to 'two weeks of online shopping' to 'three months of looking'. If you want to get technical about it, nearly 80 per cent of people who responded said that they had absolutely no regrets about what they chose for their wedding, with only 11 per cent having more complicated feelings towards it, mostly citing having to change their plans, which thus affected their final outfit choice. And the remaining minority percentage didn't like what they wore at all. These are pretty healthy and encouraging numbers to go by if we're taking this as a perspective to shop by.

So here's the catch and the most important part of approaching shopping like it's your wedding outfit: many of us don't believe that the wedding dress holds that much significance. While it may seem counterintuitive, this is the exact point I want to make. We take great care thinking about an item that we know will likely cost more than most of the clothes we've ever bought and we still don't let our wedding dress define our identity, our special day or even what marriage means. It is a beautiful piece that we value, feel gorgeous in and will be able to tell a story about. Doesn't that sound so damn sustainable? And most impressive of all, the unanimous response I get when I ask many people about their wedding dress is that they say they want something that they'd be able to wear again.

In the world of sustainability, style and all the complicated things we've delved into in this book, there are so many nuances and discrepancies. But one thing that I'm sure of is that no one stands there on the morning of their wedding day, looking into the mirror, saying, 'Why don't I have anything to wear?'

Acknowledgements

A lot of the development of the Mindful Monday Method took place in the midst of a pandemic. You could call it an accelerated degree in the fashion industry. That's what it felt like, anyway. I absorbed everything there was to learn from factory owners, buyers, fashion designers, journalists and PR people. I did field trips, took online courses and taught myself some of the dressmaking techniques I saw so that I could better understand how garments are made. I can confirm that I will not be opening up an atelier anytime soon. Sewing at a commercial level is really hard! It's a sure way to make you appreciate how even the simplest garment done well is a highly skilled task.

A key takeaway for anyone hoping to create a different path for themselves in fashion or even social media is to know that any kind of influence cannot be accomplished alone. You, my wonderful community, have connected so many individuals to this new and, may I be so bold as to claim, first programme to get us shopping better for our mental health. It's from reposting and sharing content, word of mouth, mentioning the method on Reddit threads and Twitter (platforms that at present I don't have a profile on and yet you have mentioned me, thank you!). You're part of this more than you know. The conversations we had in private messages. The pictures of clothes, documents and studies that you sent me from work. The links to articles you thought I'd find interesting. The candid information about how dark the manufacturing industry can be when you cut corners. The factory tours and design studio visits. I took it all in.

Collectively, we've established an actionable step-by-step guide to buying clothing and expressing ourselves, all while keeping a mindful eye on our environmental impact. Being more sustainable genuinely is better for our wellness and wallets. It's through connecting those dots that I believe we can actually start to make change, now.

So how does someone who has struggled so much with mental health throughout her life find herself writing acknowledgements in her first book? There were multiple times when I wanted to give up. In particular, that mental health crisis in 2019 was like a spiritual earthquake that sent shockwaves through every area of my life. When the flimsy constructions of 'success' I had built fell apart around me, I realised how much work

Acknowledgements

I needed to do on myself. Who I was isn't my job, how well I dressed or who I knew. As I embarked on the very painful journey of self-development and discovering my identity and faith, the Mindful Monday Method naturally grew alongside that.

The path isn't straight and it isn't over but at least I know where I'm going and you're always welcome to walk with me.

Endnotes

i   https://knowledge.wharton.upenn.edu
search/#t=articles&sort=relevancy &layout=card

ii   https://www2.deloitte.com/uk/en/pages/press-
releases/articles/four-out-of-five-uk-consumers-adopt-
more-sustainable-lifestyle-choices-during-covid-19-
pandemic.html

iii   http://changingmarkets.org/wp-content/
uploads/2021/07/SyntheticsAnonymous_FinalWeb.pdf

iv   https://cleanclothes.org/news/2021/workers-owed-
1185-billion-after-fashion-brands-inaction

v   https://cleanclothes.org/news/2021/workers-owed-
1185-billion-after-fashion-brands-inaction

vi   https://www.sciencedirect.com/science/article/abs/
pii/S001393512100133X

vii   https://techfundingnews.com/depop-founder-backs-
2-4m-funding-round-of-this-female-led-clothing-
alteration-app/

viii   https://clothesaid.co.uk/about-us/facts-on-clothes-recycling/

ix   https://www.salvationarmytrading.org.uk/news/wed-09232020-1737/satcol-reuses-and-recycles-over-5-million-items-each-week

x   https://www.ucl.ac.uk/anthropology/people/academic-and-teaching-staff/daniel-miller/fashion-and-anxiety

xi   This is the link: https://www.mckinsey.com/industries/retail/our-insights/state-offashion

xii   https://www.statista.com/statistics/910770/harrods-limited-turnover/#:~:text=In per cent20the per cent20financial per cent20year per cent202021,million per cent20pounds per cent20a per cent20year per cent20earlier

xiii   https://www.theindustry.fashion/liberty-london-sales-rise-to-82m-in-latest-financial-year/#:~:text=Historic per cent20London per cent20department per cent20store per cent20Liberty,million per cent20in per cent20the per cent20year per cent20prior.

xiv   https://twitter.com/Google/status/1605652241951690774?lang=en

xv   https://www.instagram.com/p/CqA9WDOIwz4/

xvi   https://www.cdc.gov/niosh/pgms/worknotify/drycleaner1.html

xvii   https://www.nytimes.com/2021/06/02/business/etsy-depop.html

xviii   https://carbonliteracy.com/climate-change-fashion-waste-colonialism/#:~:text=The%20term%20'waste%20colonialism'%2C,group%20through%20waste%20and%20pollution.

Endnotes

xix   https://link.springer.com/article/10.1007/s40521-019-0197-5

xx   https://intracen.org/sites/default/files/uploadedFiles/intracenorg/Content/Publications/Vicuna_trade_final_Low_res.pdf

xxi   www.businessoffashion.com/articles/sustainability/inside-the-business-of-vicuna-the-wool-worth-more-than-gold/

xxii www.permanentstyle.com/2021/02/behind-the-scenes-at-the-loro-piana-factory.html

xxiii https://2030.wool.com/globalassets/2030/documents/GD3821-WCG-Wool-2030-Discussion-Paper-1-5.pdf

xxiv https://www.levi.com/US/en_US/blog/article/501-renewcell

xxv   https://www.mckinsey.com/industries/retail/our-insights/state-of-fashion

xxvi https://www.fastretailing.com/eng/ir/direction/position.html

xxvii https://www.theguardian.com/money/2019/nov/30/are-things-going-wrong-with-the-uk-beloved-dr-martens-brand

xxviii https://www.ftc.gov/business-guidance/advertising-marketing/made-in-usa

About the Author

© Alise Jane

Andrea Cheong is a journalist and the founder of the Mindful Monday Method, which teaches shoppers to buy better for their mental health and the planet. She has been named one of the fashion critics to watch by *Vogue Business* and has been featured in *Harper's Bazaar* US and *Glamour* UK. Her viral lessons such as 'How to find your capsule wardrobe' and 'How to do a wardrobe audit' have been featured on *Buzzfeed* UK and *British Vogue*, respectively.